CANADA
KNITS

CANADA KNITS

CRAFT AND COMFORT IN A NORTHERN LAND

SHIRLEY A. SCOTT

Warwick Publishing Group
Toronto   Los Angeles
Toronto Montreal

CANADA KNITS
Craft and Comfort in a Northern Land

W
Warwick
Publishing
Group

Senior Supervising Editor: Susan Calvert
Senior Sponsoring Editor: Glen Ellis

Designer: Stuart Knox

Canadian Cataloguing in Publication Data

Scott, Shirley (Shirley A.)
Canada Knits

Includes bibliographical references.
ISBN 0-07-549973-8

1. Knitting – Canada. 2. Knitting – Social aspects – Canada – History. 3. Knitting – Canada – History. 4. Yarn. I. Title.

TT819.C3S28 1990 746.43'2'0971 C90-094906-6

Printed and bound in Canada

Care has been taken to trace the ownership of any copyright material contained in this text. The publishers welcome any information that will enable them to rectify, in subsequent editions, any incorrect or omitted reference or credit.

Jacket Photo Credits — *Front:* background, Photo by George Georgakakos, courtesy of the Nova Scotia Designer Crafts Council and Anne MacLeod Prado; left and right, Photos by Patons Design Studio, Book 526, courtesy of Patons & Baldwins Canada; centre, Courtesy of White Buffalo Mills. *Back:* top, Courtesy of the Whyte Museum of the Canadian Rockies, Banff, Alberta, V343/P035(1); bottom left, Courtesy of Knitwear Architects.

For My Mother

Who Taught Me To Knit

CONTENTS

CHAPTER 4 — Canada's Knitting Yarns And How We Got Them   67

CHAPTER 5 — Who Knits In Canada?   94

CHAPTER
6 Why Canadians Knit   111

ACKNOWLEDGEMENTS

A great number of people in many different parts of the Canadian knitting world gave generously of their time and energy to help make this book possible. I would like to thank each and every one of them heartily for making my work easier and more enjoyable.

Every knitter and designer who provided me with biographical information and with photographs of their work deserve extra special thanks. I hope that this book will draw attention to their talents and to their commitment to knitting as an art.

Busy people working in cultural institutions across Canada gave extra attention to my unusual request for information about knitting. Some spent a great deal of time searching unfamiliar corners of their collections for elusive photographs, often because they were knitting enthusiasts themselves. Among all those who helped in special ways, I would like to particularly acknowledge the assistance of: Linda Cobon, Canadian National Exhibition Archives; Joseph Romain, Hockey Hall of Fame; Lena Goon, Whyte Museum of the Canadian Rockies; Marijke Kerkhoven, Glenbow Museum; Birgitta Wallace, Environment Canada: Parks; Bernard Pothier, Canadian War Museum; Andrea Kirkpatrick, New Brunswick Museum; Cheryl Rielly, Canada's Sports Hall of Fame; Jacqueline Beaudoin-Ross, McCord Museum of Canadian History; Anu Liivandi-Palias, Royal Ontario Museum; the staff of Montgomery's Inn; the staff of the Public Archives of Nova Scotia and the Nova Scotia Museum Complex; the staff of the Prince Edward Island Museum and Heritage Foundation; and the staff of the National Archives of Canada. The efforts of all of these people and institutions made my work better.

I also received a great deal of help from the publishing world. The following people helped me to find information for my book and gave me permission to use it: Carole Harmon, Altitude Publishing; Doris Saunders and Judy McGrath, *Them Days* Magazine; Georgia Bent, *Up Here* Magazine; Anna Hobbs, *Canadian Living* Magazine; and Lyn Hancock.

In the craft world, I would like to particularly thank Anne Manuel of the Newfoundland and Labrador Crafts Development Association for giving me an excellent introduction to Newfoundland knitting and all the craftspeople at the Summer Craft Fair held in St. John's in July, 1989, for giving me their time. Knitters from other parts of Canada who gave me special help also deserve a vote of thanks. They include Diane Debray and Nancy Vivian, Craft Cottage, Richmond, British Columbia; Joan Warren and the staff of Village Yarns, Islington, Ontario; George Fry, New Brunswick Crafts School; Barbara Gunn and Doreen McKnight, Etobicoke, Ontario; Gerda and Fritz Anthony, Fairview, Alberta; Wendy Chambers, Whitehorse, Yukon; Patricia Freeman, Dutton, Ontario; and Marilyn Woolridge and the staff of NONIA for their time and patience in answering my sometimes difficult questions.

Many organizations answered my call for help in researching their involvement with knitting and sometimes found the quest of personal interest. These include William G. Hillaby, Navy League of Canada; Lil Greene, Ontario Voice of Women Knitting Project; Ellen Boynton, Canadian Home Economics Association; Suzanne Williams, Imperial Order Daughters of the Empire; Harold McQuatty, Dunnville District Heritage Association; and each of the provincial coordinators of the 4-H Clubs in Canada.

In the literary arena, I am indebted to the published work of other knitting historians on which I relied extensively. This includes books by Bishop Rutt, Michael Harvey, Dorothy Burnham, Janetta Dexter, Robin Hansen, Margaret Meikle, Wendy Chambers, Judy McGrath, Birgitta Wallace, Helen Bennett, Lady Veronica Gainford, and Elizabeth Zimmermann.

The corporate world also gave me great assistance. Nimble Mouse Communications, Scarborough, Ontario, and Flight Lines, Ottawa, Ontario, produced graphic materials for the book. Daryl Foster of Sasquatch Trading in Victoria, British Columbia, and Judy Hill of Hill's Indian Crafts, Koksilah, British Columbia, provided helpful information about Cowichan knitting. Campbell

Soup permitted me to use its "It's Better Than A Sweater" advertisement. Patons & Baldwins of Darlington, Co. Durham, England, kindly provided me with the picture of John Paton. Mary Maxim gave me some enjoyable hours in its archives and in its offices.

The wool industry was most attentive to my need for information. Many thanks to the Wool Bureau of Canada for permission to reproduce the story of the Woolmark label and for other assistance and to the Canadian Cooperative Wool Growers for the great wealth of information they provided. Kroy Unshrinkable Wools, Patons & Baldwins Canada, and CIBA Geigy Canada Ltd. provided me with understandable information about their highly complicated yarn processing operations. The yarn manufacturers were the kindest of all. Their hospitality, access to corporate archives, historical information, and wonderful mill tours gave me a real appreciation of their commitment to making and selling quality hand-knitting yarns.

Many knitters supplied me with information and with the older pattern books that were at the heart of Canadian knitting. Myra Blackburn of Lever Brothers Ltd. shared the corporate collection of Lux pattern books with me. Michele Urquhart of Patons & Baldwins introduced me to its collection. The names of my other most generous benefactors are Mary Oglanby, Aurora, Ontario; Mrs. H. Dawson, Ajax, Ontario; Rita Workman, Islington, Ontario; Marjorie Morrison, Cameron, Ontario; Peggy Kondals, St. Laurent, Quebec; Mrs. H. Elines, Newmarket, Ontario; Phyllis Turrell, Kingston, Ontario; Susanne Buchanan, Weston, Ontario; Vera Mews, St. John's, Newfoundland; Dr. Anna Templeton, St. John's, Newfoundland; Tony Buckle, Margaret Hambleton, Dorothy McKnight, Irene R. Schutt, and Doris Rydall, all of Toronto. These knitters gave me access to treasured books, some of which had been in their families for decades and all of which had personal meaning.

Special thanks to David Blackwood and Mila Mulroney for supplying me with images for this book and to Jock White for reading my work in progress.

I am also indebted to the Jean A. Chalmers Fund for the Crafts, Visual Arts Section, Canada Council for a grant that helped me to acquire photographs for my book.

Family and friends also did their part to help me with my work and to supply me with daily encouragement. Denise Parrott, a fellow librarian and dedicated knitter did research for me into traditional knitting in Newfoundland. Margaret Foster provided timely information about the British royal family at any and every hour of the day when it was requested. Chris Burke put me on the trail of the Queen Victoria scarf. Jane Cain provided me with a number of very helpful leads. Joan Warren's keen interest kept me believing that this book was a worthwhile endeavour. My mother-in-law, Irene Florkow of Richmond, British Columbia, and my auntie, Mrs. Edgar Payne of Bathurst, New Brunswick, kept me continually supplied with knitting facts and with family information from both sides of the country.

Mike Roy and Denise Schon have my enduring thanks for encouraging me to write this book. The greatest thanks of all goes to my husband, David Florkow, whose hard work made taking advantage of the opportunity possible.

CANADA KNITS

CHAPTER 1

How Knitting Came To Canada

Introduction

Hand knitting is a democratic, low technology flourishing of personal creativity that is alive and well in Canada today. You may knit a beautiful garment for twenty dollars or for two hundred dollars. You may knit with the fibres of science or the fibres of history. Only the simplest equipment is needed — money is no barrier to knitting. You may wear a knitted garment to a skating rink, to a bar mitzvah, or to a shareholders' meeting — knitting has social standing. You may clothe yourself or your friends, for hand knitting is an act of generosity.

Best of all, for the knitter, hand knitting is a straw into gold experience, one of the highest orders of self-fulfillment options in a complicated world. The excitement of transforming a linear filament into a work of three-dimensional wear-able art, all while sitting in your favourite chair, is hard to surpass. Knitters arrive — they are not always travelling. Knitters' eyes glitter, their fingers glide, and their minds and bodies are engaged and active. They get the best from life.

But in the beginning there was necessity.

Canada is a northern land, and except for its gentle, wave-lapped coastal regions, it is full of fire and ice. But the fire seems brief and the ice long. Our summers are short celebratory affairs for throwing away on pleasure — it is winter that grips the Canadian imagination. For all but the most insulated city dweller, winter is both a natural and a spiritual force to be reckoned with. Knitting is a remarkable weapon on both scores.

When the first Europeans came to this country, they were often shocked by the ferocity of the seasons that went along with the opportunities of life in their adopted land. Their need for warm, serviceable clothing was urgent and imperative. Canadian knitters have always had their work cut out for them.

Early Woolcraft in Canada

Despite their excellent needlework skills, native Canadians did not knit before European contact. They worked with skins, grasses, and other animal and vegetable fibres, weaving, sewing, embroidering, and ornamenting their clothing and household objects with intricate skill. In fact, one of the reasons why the first intrusive Europeans were not more positively repelled was the native people's interest in the trade goods that the Europeans brought. Their fine metal sewing needles easily replaced the more awkward bone needles and were among the earliest and most prized trade goods.

Native Canadians did, however, have some skill in woolcraft. They made use of the wool of wild animals that was shed in spring and found caught up on twigs or blowing loose across the land. Inuit women today, for example, tuck bits of qiviuq, the underdown of the musk ox, into their seal skin boots for added warmth. We may safely assume that such an opportunity for warmer feet would not have been neglected in past centuries.

We know too that the hair of domesticated dogs was used by Pacific Coast Indian tribes to make clothing and that these people also had spinning skills. Anthropologists tell us that the Salish people, who have a rich textile tradition, were skillful blenders of dog hair, duck down, and vegetable fibres, which they twisted and spun into yarns and wove into blankets. Some spinning whorls and blanket pins have been found that are two thousand years old.

The adeptness of native women at needlework, their skill in shaping garments, their love of ornamentation, and their eye for design meant that when they were finally introduced to knitting they seized upon it and became some of the most dedicated practitioners of the art.

Knitting skills were passed on to many native people at the same time as religion and the other fundamentals of European culture. The missionaries saw the teaching of knitting as a means of avoiding idleness and of building character rather than as a form of artistic expression. Nevertheless, the tools that they gave to native people were valuable indeed.

Canada's First Knitters

Canada's first knitters did not stay. The first Europeans to establish a settlement in Canada were the Norse, who came from Scandinavia via Iceland and landed at l'Anse aux Meadows on the northernmost tip of Newfoundland. They did not leave any actual knitting behind them. However, we do know that they worked with wool.

Excavators at the site of l'Anse aux Meadows have uncovered a small number of artefacts that offer a glimpse of the woolcraft of these Norse colonists. A spindle whorl of soapstone, a small needle-hone of quartzite, and an elongated bone needle were found. All of these objects are indisputably Norse and were not known to the local native Canadians of the period. They were part of a woman's tool kit. Socks and mittens were probably knit using the single-needle *nalbindning* technique, a form of knitting that predates the two-needle method. The yarn used at l'Anse aux Meadows was probably wool, although the Norse occupants did not practice agriculture here as they did in their other colonies where sheep and cattle farming dominated the economy.

The settlement at l'Anse aux Meadows was short lived. Perhaps, as Birgitta Wallace suggests in *The Norse Atlantic Saga*, it was merely a stopover point for trading voyages. The journey south may have seemed too long, the season too short, and the goods no more exotic than those easily obtained from Europe. For whatever reason, the outpost was abandoned, and with it disappeared the opportunity of leaving knitting knowledge behind.

The earliest known knitted piece found in Canada did not come from settlers at all but from seasonal workers who probably brought it with them. It is a fragment of a knitted cap found at the late sixteenth century Basque whaling site at Red Bay, Labrador. The Basque people harvested our rich coastal waters for many years before the French and the English established themselves here, but the Basques were economic opportunists, not empire builders. They were happy to return home when their work was done. Their most lasting legacy is the place names that remain on the coasts of Newfoundland and Labrador, not the art of knitting.

L'Anse aux Meadows, site of the early Norse settlement in Canada

Knitting Among the Founding Peoples

The English and the French were the first to plant themselves and their knitting firmly on Canadian soil and to put down roots.

Both France and England were true knitting cultures. In France, *corps de la bonneterie* existed from quite early times. Everyone remembers the notorious *tricoteuses* of the French Revolution who got such bad press in Charles Dickens' *A Tale of Two Cities* — French knitters have had a lot to live down. The French themselves believed that knitting came to them from Scotland, another country that had a great impact on the development of Canada and on Canadian knitting.

Nineteenth century French painting frequently portrayed needleworkers on the job. Degas' *The Millinery Shop* and Renoir's *Lady Sewing* are good examples. The tranquility, the self-containment, and the beatific expressions of women concentrating on intricate tasks clearly fascinated the more sensitive painters. Moreover, for the women involved, a modelling job probably seemed like a windfall. It was easy work and must have been financially rewarding since one neither had to move nor to stop "real" work to do it.

Knitters were also frequently painted, but usually by artists whose work is less well remembered today. The many painters who established themselves in Brittany during the nineteenth century made frequent use of knitters as a theme for developing their creative powers.[1] They saw knitting as an activity that symbolized industrious peasant life, and since Bretons are in fact Celts, closely related to the Scots and Irish, it is not surprising that all three peoples knit prolifically.

Knitting has also known a moment or two of glory among the performing arts. To France we owe the only known musical work named for knitters, a brief piece for the piano by the composer Francois Couperain (1668–1733) titled *Les tricoteuses*. It is full of sprightly stacatto notes that mimic the sound of clicking needles. We do not know whether the composer found this sound soothing or irritating, for it must be admitted that throughout history there have been rather different schools of thought on that matter.

There is clear evidence that knitting penetrated even the musicial consciousness of the French people. *Les tricoteuses* predates the French Revolution so we know that it was not written for the fabled Madame Defarge and her company, but we will likely never know which knitters were singled out for such recognition.

Richard Rutt, the Bishop of Leicester and a noted English knitting historian, generously mentions that it was France that gave us a bona fide, latter day knitting saint: Jean-Marie-Baptiste Vianney, the famous *curé* of Ars (1786–1859). As children, he and his sister tended the family flock, both of them taking their knitting with them as shepherds of either sex usually did. The saintly boy always carried a statue of the Virgin Mary with him and made a little grotto for it out of leaves and flowers. There he would often go to pray, asking his sister to knit on his stocking for him while he performed his devotions.

In the early years of the nineteenth century, it was estimated that eighty percent of the stockings made in France were knit by hand. We can therefore safely assume that the French explorers, colonists, voyageurs, *coureurs de bois*, and missionaries who came to Canada in earlier centuries wore hand-knitted stockings in the vast northern land that their countryman Voltaire dismissed as *quelques arpents de neige*.

From the time of Henry VIII onward, the English became the great knitters that they are today. Queen Elizabeth I set a fashion for knitted silk stockings and also began the long involvement of English monarchs with the hand-knitting industry. After receiving her first pair, she is claimed to have said:

> *...indeed I like silk stockings so well, because they are so pleasant, fine and delicate, that henceforth I will wear no more cloth stockings.*[2]

Beloved by her people, Queen Elizabeth I took care to protect their livelihoods. She is credited with encouraging the knitting industry of the Channel Islands, which makes her indirectly responsible for perpetuating the knitting vocabulary of "jerseys," "guernseys," and "gansies" that is still used for fishermen sweaters today. Similarly, she encouraged the makers of knitted caps by making it an offence punishable by fine for a man to appear without one except on designated days. With such royal attention business must have boomed.

Today, the English continue to distinguish themselves as knitters. Let us not forget that an Englishwoman holds the world record for knitting speed. The 1990 edition of the *Guinness Book of World Records* states that Mrs. Gwen Matthewman of West Yorkshire was clocked at 111 stitches per minute.

Our founding peoples came from solid knitting stock. After the English and French battled on the Plains of Abraham, French civilization in Canada was not replaced by English. Francophone Canadians maintained their religion, their way of life, and their native arts and crafts as did the English. The significant point for knitters is that 1759 was a military victory not a moral or cultural one, regardless of what the victorious soldiers may have thought of their day's work at the time. French and English knitters began to coexist in one country and their industrious, adaptive ways remained with them.

Two Colonial Knitters

Not many fragments of the earliest colonial knitting remain in Canadian cultural institutions, probably because the garments were designed for and received hard wear. Moreover, moth and rust doth corrupt and are at the root of many textile casualties. Happily though, some very interesting personal testimonies remain.

Two stories of newcomers to Canada tell us something about the diversity and the similarity of the colonial experience.

A Knitting Venus

Many immigrants brought skilled family servants with them. Before the abolition of slavery in the British Empire, these servants were sometimes slaves.

In the late 1930s, the Nova Scotia writer Clara Dennis published a valuable record of the history of her province as told by the Nova Scotians she interviewed. She spoke with an elderly black man, then living in Shelburne County, whose grandparents had been brought to Nova Scotia from the southern United States as slaves, possibly with Loyalist masters. The fact that Canada had given his grandparents freedom remained an important part of this man's consciousness.

His grandparents were named Jupiter and Venus. After Venus gained her freedom in Canada, she not only cared for her own large family and lived the difficult life of a settler in a rugged land but worked "by the day" as well. And it seems that, more than anything else, the family remembered Venus as a prodigious knitter who bought wool, carded and spun it, and made countless socks, not only for her own people but also to sell.

These few tantalizing details are all we know of Venus the knitter, one personality sketched in detail from among the thousands of colonists that made Canada what it is today. One wonders if she ever knit with cotton in her far off southern home.

Roughing It in the Bush

Not all immigrants arrived in Canada with all the necessary pioneer skills and settled gratefully into their new life. Susanna Moodie, in her memoir, *Roughing It in the Bush, or, Life in Canada*, chronicles the physical and psychological hardships that a gentlewoman experienced in the Canadian wilderness in the early nineteenth century.

Susanna Moodie was a capable needlewoman and described her well-ordered work basket with pride. She wrote:

I was at work, and my workbox was open upon the table, well stored with threads and spools of all descriptions.[3]

Surprising though it may seem, Susanna did not knit; nor did she know how to make bread, an equally life-threatening problem. While she did learn to make bread, she never learned to knit and that deficiency gave her a literary opportunity to expose the brazen behaviour of the native born Canadian — and provide today's knitters with a very amusing anecdote. She wrote:

The [serving] boy was without socks, and I sent him to old Mrs. H ——— , to inquire of her what she would charge for knitting him two pairs of socks. The reply was, a dollar. This was agreed to, and dear enough they were; but the weather was very cold, and the lad was barefooted, and there was no alternative

than either to accept her offer, or for him to go without.

In a few days, Monaghan brought them home; but I found upon inspecting them that they were old socks new-footed. This was rather too glaring a cheat, and I sent the lad back with them, and told him to inform Mrs. H ——— that as he had agreed to give the price for new socks, he expected them to be new altogether.[4]

We are indebted to Susanna Moodie for a fascinating personal view of the tribulations of early colonial life in Canada.

She also left us some of the most fearsome and convincing descriptions of cold weather ever put on paper. On one occasion she wrote:

...the heavens shone brightly but the cold was so severe that every article of food had to be thawed before we could get our breakfast. The very blankets that covered us during the night were stiff with our frozen breath.[5]

One wonders how the Moodies could have been so unprepared for the Canadian climate but, to a Briton, Canada's cold could not possibly be imagined. Susanna wrote that the following "extempore ditty" was composed by her husband during the first very cold night they spent in Canada:

Oh, the cold of Canada nobody knows,
The fire burns our shoes without warming
    our toes;
Oh, dear, what shall we do?
Our blankets are thin, and our noses are
    blue —
Our noses are blue, and our blankets are
    thin,
It's zero without, and we're freezing within!
(Chorus). Oh, dear, what shall we do? etc.[6]

Humour and spirit undoubtedly helped to generate as much warmth as did knitting in colonial Canada.

CHAPTER 2

Heritage Knitters From Sea To Sea To Sea

Since colonial times Canadians have taken up their needles in every province and territory of Canada. We have world renowned knitters on our Atlantic, Pacific, and Northern coasts. The Cowichan Indians of British Columbia have made their famous sweaters since the middle of the nineteenth century. On the Atlantic coast, the knitters of NONIA, the Newfoundland Outport Nursing and Industrial Association, celebrated their seventieth anniversary in 1990. In Labrador, knitters for the Grenfell Mission continue a movement that began in 1906. All are thriving businesses that have taken the good news of Canadian knitting to the rest of the world. They are heritage knitters whose methods, materials, and patterns are deeply rooted in history and tradition, yet their work is adaptable and always fresh. They link our knitting present to our rich knitting past.

With Labour and With Art: The Story of Cowichan Knitting

There are many interesting stories about the origins of the Cowichan Indian knitting of British Columbia. Some suggest that it was learned from Scottish settlers, perhaps even from Scotsmen, not women. Others think that the wives of Japanese fishermen employed in the coastal fishery may have taught some Cowichan people to knit. Still others say that missionaries were largely responsible. No one knows for certain.

Like Canada itself, the Cowichan sweater is a multicultural product whose precise beginnings may be impossible to pinpoint. Once thought of as a rugged uniform for the fishermen, loggers, and hunters of British Columbia, it is now a highly praised international fashion symbol that makes people everywhere think of Canada.

With more than two thousand members, the Cowichan Band is the largest of British Columbia's Indian bands. Its centre is in the Cowichan Valley area of Vancouver Island, near the town of Duncan. It forms part of the Coast Salish nation, whose history on Vancouver Island goes back nearly ten thousand years.

In the late 1700s, white explorers came to this area; and nearly a century later, knitting was introduced. The Cowichan sweater is a product of these times.

The Sisters of St. Ann

Knitting and industry seem to go together. This fact was not lost on the early missionaries who came to Canada. They passed their knitting skills on to others.

The Cowichan people were on the receiving end of an extra portion of missionary zeal in realms other than the spiritual. Most people believe that it was the Sisters of St. Ann who gave the Cowichan people the fundamentals of knitting and taught them to make socks, mittens, long underwear, and possibly even plain sweaters.

Textile writer Wendy Chambers, herself a native of the town of Duncan, tells us that Indian girls and women began receiving formal instruction in knitting with the arrival of the Sisters of St. Ann in 1864, the Church of England Mission in 1865, and the appointment of William Lomas as teacher and Indian catechist in 1867. These were formative years indeed.

Margaret Meikle, a textile historian and curator of a unique 1987 exhibition on Cowichan knitting sponsored by the B.C. Museum of Anthropology, adds that mission records tell of students' knitting being displayed at local fairs and at the Chicago World's Fair in 1893.

After basic knitting skills were learned, it was another twenty or more years before Jeremina Colvin, a Scottish settler, taught the Indians to knit their first patterned sweaters, using the Fair Isle method.

Jeremina Colvin's Gift

Jeremina Colvin, née Robertson, was born on July 9, 1859, in a crofter's cottage in the Parish of Tingwall, on the Shetland Islands of Scotland. Knitting was in her blood. She told her son Magnus that she could not remember a time when she did not know how to spin and knit. She had learned to spin when she was so young that she had to stand to reach the foot lever on the wheel.

In 1885, Jeremina emigrated to Canada, bringing her energy and considerable skill with her. She met and married Robert Mouat Colvin, and the two homesteaded at Cowichan Station. Like many other newcomers, the life that faced Jeremina was an immense change. Much of Vancouver Island was still wilderness. As one writer described it:

> The Esquimalt and Nanaimo Railway was not yet built: travel was by horse and wagon or ox cart over rough bush trails. Bear and cougar and wolves were plentiful. Even children carried guns to school and knew how to use them.[7]

Neighbours were treasures in the new country, and Jeremina befriended the native women whose husbands helped the Colvins to clear their land. When the land was ready, the Colvins began to raise sheep. Jeremina knit much of the family clothing with their wool. The barter system was often the only way to get necessities in pioneer societies, and she may have exchanged some garments for fish, baskets, and other useful goods provided by the native people.

Two Cowichan women asked Jeremina to teach them to knit so that they could make garments to keep their men warm when they were on the sea, working in the bush, or hunting. Then, in the time tested "each one teach one" manner, these women passed on the skill to their daughters and neighbours. What began as a personal exchange to satisfy an individual need eventually grew into an important community-based industry.

Jeremina taught the traditional circular method of construction, which was the style of the Shetland "jumpers" she had learned to knit as a child. (Circular knitting remains a distinguishing feature of genuine Cowichan sweaters today.) The first stitch patterns were classic Fair Isle designs — the clever combinations of "oxo" motifs separated by narrow bands of small repeating "peerie" patterns, all worked by stranding the two colours of yarn as one progressed. The result was an impressive and fresh New World look with Old World familiarity.

As the expertise of the native women grew, their artistic impulse also grew. They began to develop their own patterns using symbols from their own culture, but they maintained the practical Shetland method of circular construction and never entirely abandoned Shetland pattern motifs. Jeremina's legacy of skill was enriched by the vision, talent, and individuality of later creators. This is a teacher's greatest reward.

The Materials of Cowichan Knitting

The materials of Cowichan knitting have not changed from Jeremina's time to our own. Cowichan knitters prefer wooden needles for their work because the wool that they work with is so heavy. Up to nine of these are used at one time when the knitter reaches the widest part of the garment.

Anthropologist Barbara Lane analysed these knitting needles in detail when she did field work among the Cowichan Band in the late 1940s.

Lane wrote that the varieties of wood most commonly used for needles were dogwood, iron-wood, vine maple, ninebark, and yellow cedar. Making them required many steps. First, the wood was cut in two-foot lengths and slowly dried for several months. Then, these long pieces of wood were split into strips that measured about 1 inch by 1 1/2 inches. These smaller strips were bound with cord so that they would not bend or warp and were dried for another month. During this time, the cord was continually tightened to prevent bending.

A wood file was used to shape the pieces into needles about 11 inches long and 1/4 inch thick with tapered ends, roughly the equivalent of a 6 mm needle today. Finally, the needles were smoothed with sandpaper. Lane added that a plant known as scouring rush and the rough skin of the dogfish were also used for sanding.

A genuine Cowichan sweater is knit from thick, single-ply, handspun wool in natural colours. This distinguishes it from other sweaters and from its imitators.

The Coast Salish people had well-developed textile skills before they began using the wool of sheep for knitting. For example, the hair of wild

Young knitters on the Cowichan Reserve, circa 1960.

mountain goats and domesticated dogs were both used in weaving, often combined with vegetable fibre and even duck down.

Before European contact, the Coast Salish people domesticated a breed of small, white, long-haired dog called the Salish Wool Dog. These wool dogs disappeared after cross breeding with animals brought by the Europeans, but by that time they were no longer necessary because the settlers had brought sheep with them.

According to Lane, sheep were imported from England and California to Puget Sound between 1839 and 1840 and were probably introduced to Vancouver Island about the same time. The Hudson Bay Company employed the first farmers and the first flockmasters on the Island. Most of the early settlers and Bay employees on the island came from the Scottish highlands and islands, sheep raising districts par excellence, and they found the land and climate most agreeable for this familiar form of agriculture. Sheep's wool alone has been used for making Cowichan sweaters since then.

The Hudson Bay Company did not follow the common practice of destroying black lambs, but used them as breeding stock. Today, black wool is much prized. One writer described it this way:

The black sheep begins life as a coal black lamb, but grows rusty brown, then grizzled grey as it ages. All stages of the wool are used in the Cowichan sweaters but the crisp black on clear white fetches the highest prices from the tourists. The grey or brownish sweaters are more popular with working men, since they need not be washed so often. Washing has a tendency to destroy their wind and rain resisting qualities but does not affect their durability.[8]

In days gone by, the wool was prepared entirely by hand, using the traditional, labour-intensive methods of hand washing, carding, and spinning. Many interesting photographic reminders of these preparations remain, particularly of the ingenious home-made machinery contrived to simplify these tasks. Meikle reports that some knitters still buy shorn fleeces and use traditional methods of preparation. But most buy the washed and carded wool directly from a commercial carding mill such as Modeste's on the Koksilah reserve near Duncan and spin it themselves.

Wonderful wool it is — soft, thick, lightly oiled, and water resistant. Its warmth is legendary, and owners of Cowichan sweaters become very attached to them. Meikle tells the story of a gen-tleman who served with the Princess Patricia's Canadian Light Infantry in Europe during World War II. He asked his wife to mail him the Cowichan sweater his parents had given him more than ten years earlier, but to remove the collar so that he could wear it under his uniform without it being detected. When he returned home his wife stitched the collar back on, and he continued to wear his sweater with pleasure and satisfaction. It not only saw action in World War II but also served the wearer well while engaged in building bridges, repairing the Alaska Highway in the Yukon, and working through the cold winters of Manitoba and Northern B.C. It is still being worn today. In the era of the throwaway economy, this is indeed a remarkable product endorsement.

Knitting Method

The method of knitting a Cowichan sweater is distinctive and sets it apart from its imitators. Pullovers and vests are knit in a circle to the armholes, then the front and back are each completed separately. Cardigans are knit in one piece from one front opening to the other to the armholes, then both fronts and the back are finished separately. A zipper fastener is sewn in later.

Shoulder seams are knit together and the stitches of the back neck are reserved for part of the collar. Today most sweaters have a shawl collar, which is knit in garter stitch, basket stitch, or ribbing. The stitches for the sleeve are picked up around the circumference of the armhole and knit downward to the ribbed cuff.

The method is a simple one, but there are no shortcuts. Design compromises like knitting sleeves separately and sewing them in later are not characteristic of the genuine Cowichan sweater.

Pattern Motifs

Cowichan knitters are as inventive as knitters anywhere in the world, and their pattern sources are equally diverse. Some interesting patterns are based on aboriginal basketry designs, but, in the way of all knitters, other motifs have been taken from everyday items of household decor like curtains, embroideries, and floor coverings.

Knitters collect and keep their designs, sometimes passing them down within a family, but there is no explicit control over who knits what. All agree that patterns are chosen for their artistic appeal, not for special symbolic or spiritual significance.

This photograph of an attractive native woman appears
on some brochures advertising Cowichan sweaters to the
Japanese.

A fine array of sweaters sold by the Cowichan Trading Company.

In today's rich world of graphic design, the potential sources of inspiration are numberless, but it takes the skill of the knitter to transform them into wearable art.

Building the Cowichan Sweater Industry

Artistic considerations aside, substantial business acumen was needed to develop a collective pastime into the magnificent, well-known industry that it is today.

How did the Cowichan knitting industry begin to grow? The Cowichan Band had plenty of contact with people of different cultures who worked on the fishing boats and in the canneries of the west coast. Its knitted garments were much admired and became a small "cash crop."

We are told that the sweaters first came to notice around 1905, when they were knit by four women in the now abandoned stone church on the reserve near Duncan. Chambers suggests that the growth of sport fishing in Cowichan Bay after World War I boosted demand significantly. In the 1920s, a man's sweater could be bought directly from a knitter for about fifteen dollars. By the late 1930s about five hundred sweaters per year were sold, and intermediaries had stepped in to retail the garments to a wider market. By 1965, six hundred knitters were producing more than 10,000 sweaters per year, selling at an average price of thirty-five dollars. Orders came from Japan, India, Britain, Europe, and the United States. A Japanese rage for them crested in the mid-1970s, bringing demand to unprecedented levels. The Japanese continue to be a lively market and many special efforts are made to attract them.

Non-native buyers were quick to see the commercial potential of Cowichan knitting and have been active in the industry since the 1930s. They buy sweaters directly from knitters, sometimes using finished chest measurement as a basic pricing guide. Some buyers also provide knitters with wool. One buyer claimed he bought his first sweater in 1930 for three dollars and turned a handsome profit by selling it to a cold-hating Chinese cook immediately after. With talents like this at work, the industry grew by leaps and bounds. Today, some third generation retailers continue to carry on their family businesses.

Retail stores in Duncan, Victoria, and Vancouver have been selling Cowichan sweaters since the 1920s. They were originally sold in sporting goods stores as outfits for hunting and fishing, but today are stocked by sophisticated craft shops, boutiques, and department stores. There is also a thriving mail-order business that can bring a Cowichan sweater to your door in days. Worldwide they are a highly esteemed and uniquely Canadian craft.

One particularly successful form of publicity for Cowichan knitting was to have famous people photographed wearing superb sweaters, much like having an athlete endorse a product today.

Cowichan sweaters have been worn by everyone from Australian ranchers to royalty. Olive and John Diefenbaker wore theirs one frosty day while planting bulbs on their Ottawa lawn, and photographers were there to record the event. Bing Crosby had a sweater made especially for him by Mrs. Pat Charlie. The back of the garment had a unique design of musical notes and the words "Chief Thunder Voice."

When Edward, Prince of Wales, himself a great fashion plate, paid a visit to Canada, he is said to have startled his valet with one of the "barbaric-looking" garments. It was made for him by the late Mary Anne Modeste, one of the best known Cowichan knitters.

Queen Elizabeth and Prince Philip had sweaters presented to them on a visit to Nanaimo, B.C., in 1959.

The Diefenbakers planting bulbs wearing their Cowichan sweaters, Ottawa, 1957.

Queen Elizabeth and Prince Philip receiving sweaters, compliments of Mrs. Elsie Bob.

For the royal wedding of Prince Charles to Lady Diana Spencer in 1982, the British Columbia government asked Marjorie Peter of Duncan, B.C., to make the province's official wedding gift. The gift of the sweaters was reported for the benefit of knitters by Anna Hobbs in *Canadian Living Magazine.* When the government approached Mrs. Peter, they asked her to work up several patterns to choose from. From these, they selected a fine geometric design. The two sweaters were similar, but not identical because the knitter takes special pride in making each sweater unique. When

asked at the time how she felt about her assignment, Mrs. Peter said, "I hope they wear their sweaters in good health and are kept warm and happy for many years to come."

Not every famous wearer of a Cowichan sweater has been blessed with such kind words. Harold Wilson, a former prime minister of Britain, was given a sweater in 1966 and was photographed wearing it while playing golf. Mr. Wilson may have been trying to imitate an earlier, famous picture of Edward, Prince of Wales playing golf in his Fair Isle sweater; a photo that started a great fashion rage for sporting sweaters. On the other hand, he might simply have been trying to keep warm and dry on a damp day. In a fit of pique, one brutal British fashion commentator described it as a "hideously patterned tummy warmer."

Maintaining the integrity and market position of genuine Cowichan sweaters is a challenge today. There are many imitators.

An admiring home knitter can easily duplicate the patterns and construction method of a Cowichan sweater, and many companies provide patterns and wool for those who are unable to work the details out themselves. The materials, however, would never be quite the same nor would the resulting garment.

A more serious problem for the industry is competition from large-scale commercial enterprises that attempt to imitate Cowichan sweaters and sell them as "Indian sweaters." Concern over this type of competition caused the Cowichan Band to take steps to protect its name legally. Today, true Cowichan sweaters are accompanied by a signed certificate of authenticity. There remains a serious need to educate the buying public about the distinctive features of genuine sweaters, their history, and their value.

After all is said and done, the uniqueness of Cowichan knitting embraces the whole tradition. Imitating certain techniques, patterns, or materials, as important as these may be, does not produce a Cowichan sweater. Making or buying a look-alike garment misses the point and merely satisfies the acquisitive motive above all else. The uniqueness of Cowichan knitting lies in every aspect of its cultural heritage, its history, the source and quality of the wool, the knitter, the place where it was knit, and in the continuity of it all. It is an enduring expression of our Canadian knitting heritage.

LOOK FOR THIS LABEL

GENUINE

COWICHAN INDIAN KNIT

HAND SPUN
CA07207
REGISTRATION
NUMBER _____

HAND KNIT
WOOL 100% LAINE

10 YEAR GUARANTEE
ON ZIPPER AND INSTALLATION

COWICHAN
SIZE _____ LADIES _____

CHILD _____ MENS _____

PRICE _____ POCKETS ☐

A certificate guaranteeing the authenticity of a Cowichan sweater.

Knitting Missions on Canada's East Coast

Missionaries sowed their seeds of skill on Canada's eastern and northern shores, as well as on the Pacific coast. Like their west coast counterparts, they did not teach spiritual things alone. They took a practical view of the material needs of their flock.

The Moravian Church was one of these. A pre-Reformation sect of free thinkers, the church was formed in the early fifteenth century. The original

Ellen Hettasch's sewing class, Nain, Labrador

church was heavily persecuted, and members took refuge in a remote part of Moravia. However, by the eighteenth century, its centre had moved to what is now Germany. Members of the Moravian Church established their first Canadian mission at Nain, Labrador, in 1771. Congregations are still active in Labrador today.

Knitting was part of the missionary contribution. Native girls were taught to knit using the left-hand throw method of yarn control, indicative of the church's European roots. Many of the mitten patterns knit in Labrador today can be linked to the patterns of Europe.

With the first visit of Sir Wilfred Grenfell in 1892, the coasts of Newfoundland and Labrador received a magnificent blessing that continues today. A man of boundless energy as well as firm beliefs, Grenfell was a medical doctor who felt a personal responsibility for the quality of life of the people he served, and he had the means to make a difference.

As head of the Grenfell Mission, with headquarters in St. Anthony, Newfoundland, Sir Wilfred established much needed hospitals, nursing stations, schools, and orphanages. He also established many "industries" as he called them, not manufacturing industries as we think of them today, but small businesses that made profitable use of people's time and talents. "Industrial workers," as they were known, took a special interest in teaching and reviving traditional handcrafts. They supplied materials and instruction when needed. The hand-made items were collected and later sold to generate income for the mission.

One Labrador woman remembered earlier days this way:

> Mom used to have wool come from St. Anthony, from the Grenfell Mission, and you could buy it from the Hudson's Bay Company ...it was old-fashioned wool, big hanks of it. We used to knit mitts and socks and stuff like that. Some people used to knit underwear. 'Twas kind of rough!...We knit fancy patterns with small wool but not on coarse work. Oh no, we never bothered about that for coarse work because we had to handle so much wool. The fancy patterns, that was for Mrs. Keddie.
>
> Mrs. Keddie was an old lady on the Grenfell Mission. She used to give us a stock of yarn...to work. It wasn't something you'd pick up all day, just sometimes. ... [Mrs. Keddie] was real particular. If it wasn't done very good you wouldn't get a very good price for your work, but if 'twas done good you got a better price.[9]

Mrs. Keddie obviously had the unenviable job of ensuring quality control in a home-based industry.

Grenfell Handicrafts was begun by Dr. Grenfell in 1906, and a continuation of this company was re-established in St. Anthony in 1984. Canadians today can buy wonderful, carefully made items with a real history to them. The company employs six full-time people and more than one hundred home workers.

Perhaps Dr. Grenfell's thoughts about practical Christianity and its role in improving individual lives were shared by all knitting missionaries. At the turn of the century, he wrote, "Religion is expressing itself in these days not so much in sentiment and the sentimental giving of dollars, as in sincere effort to...make life worthwhile."[10]

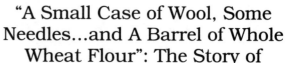

"A Small Case of Wool, Some Needles...and A Barrel of Whole Wheat Flour": The Story of NONIA of Newfoundland

The missionary spirit is not confined to religious people alone. In fact, the desire to help the less fortunate is deep and wide. Medical work is a true expression of this desire.

Newfoundland holds a unique place in the history of Canada as the place where knitting paid for nursing. In the early years of this century, there were few doctors and nurses on the island of Newfoundland, and the population suffered terribly because of the shortage. A lack of skilled midwives meant that things were particularly bad for women, and many people remember difficult births in difficult circumstances.

The Birth of NONIA

The need for an organized system of medical care on the rugged island caught the attention of Lady Harris, the wife of Sir Alexander Harris, then governor of Newfoundland. Being a decisive woman, on May 27, 1920, a ways and means committee was struck. Because there was no supply of local nurses, the committee thought it expedient to hire some experienced English nurses. By 1921, five midwives were at work in isolated outport communities.

When her husband's term expired, Lady Harris left Newfoundland and the new governor's wife, Lady Allardyce, took charge. She conceived the admirable notion that the Outport Nursing Service, as it was then called, could be made virtually self-supporting by the sale of craft items, thereby guaranteeing its future. Lady Allardyce made the inspiration for her plan clear:

I had made enquiries as to the methods followed in organizing the knitting in the Fayre Isles and Shetland, believing that there must be equal possibilities in Britain's oldest colony...the Committee sanctioned the purchase of Shetland garments as samples and patterns. Keen interest was aroused, and the urgent need for some such work in Fortune Bay gave us courage to send out our first wool.[11]

Dr. Wilfred Grenfell lent the services of one of his trained industrial workers and on August 11, 1922, Miss Minnie Pike of Red Bay, Labrador, the place where the earliest piece of knitting in Canada was found many decades later, set out "armed with a small case of wool, some needles, some Shetland garments as patterns and a barrel of whole wheat flour." History records that the first samples of knitting and weaving reached Lady Allardyce on September 29, "some hopeful, some pathetic, but all proving that these isolated people were eager to help themselves."[12]

With the profits, the nursing service grew quickly, and on January 24, 1924, a constitution was drawn up for the "Newfoundland Outport Nursing and Industrial Association." NONIA was chosen as the cable address and the registered trademark for industrial work. Its motto was "Born to Serve." By 1925, NONIA had 615 workers in thirty-five centres across the island.

NONIA and the Royals

It must be remembered that Newfoundland remained a colony of Britain until it joined the Canadian Confederation in 1949 and that connections with the motherland were stronger than with the mainland. A London branch of NONIA was established early on to help with the recruiting of British nurses and to raise the profile of the organization abroad. Through the efforts of the London Committee, members of the royal family were invited to various exhibitions of NONIA work from time to time and grew to be faithful patrons of Newfoundland crafts.

In 1927, a competition was held for the best knitted baby garments for the tiny Princess Elizabeth. Of the garments sent to Buckingham Palace, two from Newfoundland were chosen by the Queen. We do not have pictures of the prize-winning knits, but we do know that the winners' names were Miss Ethel Brown, who contributed a coat, and Mrs. Tessier, who made a bonnet.

In 1937, the present Queen Mother bought twenty-seven yards of NONIA hand-woven tweed to be made into coats for the two little princesses, Elizabeth and Margaret Rose, at one particular exhibition. It was at this time that NONIA was given permission to use the words "As supplied to Her Majesty the Queen." The articles were delivered to Buckingham Palace by Lady Allardyce, who wrote,

I do wish the Newfoundland workers could have seen and heard the Queen. She was so deeply and sincerely interested, so appreciative of the workmanship and eager to help them practically with suggestions and ideas.[13]

Such woman-to-woman communication must have cheered the workers' hearts.

Other royals have worn NONIA garments. At the same exhibition, the Duke of Kent bought two sweaters for the then Prince Edward and Princess Alexandra; and all four children of the present Queen have worn NONIA sweaters.

The NONIA Casket

When Lady Allardyce left Newfoundland in 1928, she was presented with a silver jewel casket "engraved on the cover with a loom and on the front with a map of Newfoundland on which the NONIA centres were marked in enamel, a replica of the Monarch of the Topsails, and inscribed with words of dedication."[14]

What is the Monarch of the Topsails? It is no less than the mighty caribou, the emblem of the courageous Newfoundland Regiment in World War I. The Topsails are a range of mountains in central Newfoundland, and the plentiful caribou have always been associated with the island. This rather grand name may be a deliberate echo of the famous Scottish drawing room picture of a magnificent stag, titled "Monarch of the Glen." Today, NONIA's most famous knitted item is a sweater with a caribou motif. It is its pride and joy and has been a popular design for nearly fifty years.

The jewel casket has an interesting history. The Allardyces had no family, so at the time of their deaths some of their possessions found their way into antique shops in London. About ten years ago, NONIA received a call from an Air Canada pilot living in Burlington, Ontario. He had been on the Newfoundland run for years, so he knew NONIA and its story. When poking around the

Portebello market in London, the word "NONIA" on a jewel box startled him. He enquired about it and paid a 10 pound sterling deposit on it, knowing he would be back soon. When he returned to Canada, he contacted NONIA personnel who knew instantly that it was Lady Allardyce's gift. NONIA has always had wonderful friends, and in no time at all the casket was purchased and the pilot reimbursed. Today, the casket is on display in the NONIA shop in St. John's.

NONIA Nurses

The knitting arm of NONIA went from strength to strength. What of the nursing arm?

Being a nurse in Newfoundland meant living a life that counted. Nowhere is the story of the NONIA nurses told better than in the biography of Myra Bennett, *Don't Have Your Baby in the Dory!* The book reads like a heroic saga from another century. In a sense, the provocative title sums up Myra's entire experience — the risks, the fears, and the exhausting travel on land and sea that went along with her work, as well as the terribly urgent human need for medical care.

One of the five original nurses hired by Lady Harris in 1921, Myra was a committed and energetic woman who remained active in her profession until she was past eighty years of age. She married a local fellow, Angus Bennett, after she had been in Newfoundland scarcely a year, and from that time forward considered it home. When asked why she had married so quickly she replied, "It was the only way to keep from freezing to death!"[15]

Life in Newfoundland must have seemed exotic and strange to a city-bred Englishwoman like Myra. She herself said that the two things she found most difficult to adjust to in the early years were "the smell of the dog harness hung up behind her kitchen stove and to sleep with one ear open."[16]

Although she did all sorts of general medicine, including a great deal of dentistry (Myra estimated that she pulled between three thousand and four thousand teeth during her career), midwifery was her specialty. As she herself put it, "no one will ever know what some of these women have gone through up here."[17] To complicate things, she herself was sometimes pregnant when she made her epic lifesaving journeys.

Myra the nurse was also Myra the knitter. She already knew how to knit when she came to Newfoundland but took to the local arts and crafts at once. She learned how to shear sheep and to wash, card, and dye wool. She gained particular renown for her skill as a hand spinner. In writing for an English publication in her early years, she told the following amusing story.

The spinning wheel was a permanent piece of household furniture at that time and the girls would all learn the art of spinning from their mothers who were invariably expert. In every home knitting needles and spun yarns were always in evidence and even the smallest of the girls would have a sock or a mitt "in the knit" at all times. I remember on one occasion I was attending a maternity case some miles away from home. It was a first baby and didn't seem to be in any particular hurry to arrive...so we got to work.

The father-in-law [of the pregnant woman] was a fisherman who needed new mitts, so out came the bag of wool. It was in the rough stage, meaning that it had merely been shorn from the sheep, washed and teased out. The mother-in-law now carded with two wooden "cards"...these are pulled against each other over a portion of the rough wool, thus tearing the fibres straight and forming a roll of more or less straight fibres. These rolls were then passed to me and I would spin them into yarn with the small foot-propelled spinning wheel. As soon as the yarn was ready, one of the younger girls commenced to knit the mitts and during that night of waiting, a brand new pair of mitts were completed for the thankful father.[18]

At the same time, the women also cooked a delicious beef and rabbit stew, which simmered away as the group laboured, each at her own task. In the morning, a perfectly beautiful baby was born. This incident remained one of Myra's happiest memories, taking the sting out of some of the less happy ones.

NONIA Today

NONIA has been in continuous operation since its beginning, but there have been many changes during the years. Things were particularly difficult during the depression, when sales of NONIA articles suffered greatly. In 1934, the health and handcraft functions split, and the government assumed control of the nursing service. It is as a handcraft organization that NONIA thrives today.

There were also boom times. During World War II, a number of American military bases were established in Newfoundland, and the servicemen made excellent customers. By 1946, sales of work had soared to $50,000 for the first time. There were more than seven hundred knitters and weavers at work in forty centres.

Before Confederation, NONIA had enjoyed many privileges. Postage and telegraph service were free, and there was no duty on imports of wool from England. Its special status vanished when Newfoundland became a province in 1949. In the eyes of the government, it became an organization like any other, obliged to make its way in a tough business climate. Government officials probably did not know of NONIA's unique contribution to Canada's knitting heritage.

Today, NONIA has about four hundred home workers, most of whom are knitters. They live throughout the island of Newfoundland. All knitters work at their own speed and knit whatever patterns they prefer. Their work is collected monthly. While some yarn is bought in Canada, all double-knitting wool still comes directly from England. NONIA remains in its original location on Water Street in downtown St. John's, a wonderfully historic and beautiful retail environment.

By 1981, eleven women who began working for NONIA as girls had received gold watches for fifty years of devoted knitting. One veteran talked about her early years with the association and the changes that it had brought about in her knitting style. Most Newfoundland women are "cradle to grave" knitters who intuitively know how to shape and work a garment in traditional ways. Reading a pattern and working to standard size and stitch requirements were all new skills. She explained:

> *I did know how to knit, but not the NONIA way. NONIA would send out a typed copy of the instructions and tell you the size they wanted. We enjoyed the knitting and we always had a dollar on hand when we needed the nurse.*
>
> *The [industrial] centre was a sort of quality control. When the knitting came in I would inspect it, and if it was not just right I would send it back with the instructions as to how to improve it. This is how NONIA has managed to keep such a high standard.*
>
> *There was another advantage, too. The pattern would come out and it would be so lovely that my four girls wanted garments like it. They got interested in the patterns and soon they were able to knit for themselves.... Watching the girls knit and being able to dress them beautifully gave me more pleasure than anything else.*[19]

In 1990, NONIA celebrated its seventieth anniversary, surely a unique milestone in Canadian knitting history.

CHAPTER 3

What Canadians Knit

Traditional Knitting in Canada

To knit a traditional garment in a traditional way with no printed pattern or instructions is to participate in our rapidly vanishing folk culture.

Mittens by the Millions

Mitten knitting is an international cultural phenomenon. After socks and hats, the making of mittens must surely be the most broadly-based knitting tradition in the world. After all, socks and hats are also needed in warm climates, but mittens are only necessary in the more extreme parallels of latitude. And Canadians knit them by the millions.

In Scotland, we are told, a gentleman in Highland dress was not considered properly outfitted until he donned his elegantly patterned, hand-

knit kilt hose. Machine knits were considered disgraceful and their wearers disreputable and obviously uncared for. In fact, Lady Veronica Gainford, an authority on the subject, wrote that young women sometimes performed great feats of emergency knitting to save the social reputation of less fortunate house guests who arrived with only machine-knit hose. In Canada, similar stories of knitting derring-do are told, but the subject of them is more often mittens — mittens knitted for a stranger during an hour's conversation, mittens knit to be worn home when a pair were lost in a storm, mittens knit while waiting for a baby to be born, and so on. Mitten knitting in Canada sometimes accompanied life's most important experiences.

In fact, in Canada mittens may make the man. David Blackwood's image titled "Uncle Sam Kelloway, 1876–1971" does not show a man's portrait as we might expect. Instead, it shows a pair of traditional fisherman's finger mitts laid on a bare table. Blackwood reflects on the power of symbols in a traditional culture:

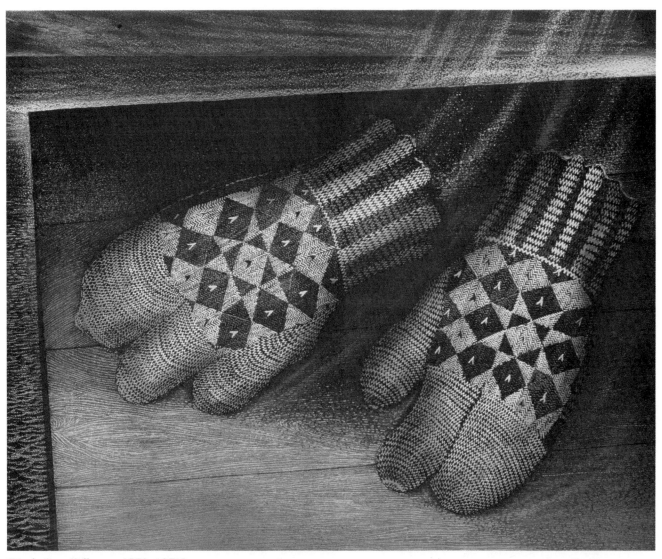

"Uncle Sam Kelloway, 1876–1971"

...[the picture] "Uncle Sam Kelloway"...tells us about Uncle Sam, through the print of his cuffs, or mitts. The design of diamonds with the little arrow shapes holds shades of windows, of paint that keeps the devil from a fishing shed; the way the fingers are planned show the way nets must be handled, the worn wood of the cutting table where the mitts are placed is vital; the way the mitts are arranged tells us about the person who placed them there. The scuff marks scraped across the table, the glow around the edge are particular and driven by an inner light. Without ever having seen Uncle Sam, we know about him and his life.[20]

A whole personality is recorded in the sensitive rendering of a humble pair of mittens.

In a lighter vein, according to the *Dictionary of Newfoundland English*, the word "cuffs" is commonly used to mean mitts. In one version of the lively and humorous song called "The Killigrews Soiree," the songwriter describes the refreshments served at what must have been a most interesting evening party. The reader will remember that not only had they "birch rine, tar twine, cherry wine and turpentine" to drink, but to eat,

> We had boiled duffs, cold duffs,
> And sugar boiled in knitted cuffs.[21]

If duffs are puddings and cuffs are mittens, it must have been a remarkable evening indeed. Note, too, that while knitters are sometimes accused of being the ultimate opportunists, snatching patterns from here and there, rhymers are perhaps even more so.

Double-Knit Mittens

Some of Canada's mittens have had their histories formally recorded. Janetta Dexter, a Nova Scotian, began to focus public attention on mitten traditions in 1972, when she was asked to demonstrate knitting at the Western Nova Scotia Arts and Crafts Association's exhibition and sale. She made a pair of mittens in a double-knitting pattern that she had learned from her grandmother. Other women who attended the demonstration were intrigued and contributed patterns that they remembered. This was the beginning of Janetta's work. Later, when she had collected enough patterns, she prepared a small booklet that was subsequently enlarged and published by the Nova Scotia Museum.

In 1986, Janetta teamed up with Robin Hansen, an American knitter and textile historian, to produce *Flying Geese & Partridge Feet: More Mittens From Up North & Down East*, another treasury of history, information, and useful patterns. Hansen had previously authored the equally important mitten book titled *Fox & Geese & Fences*, which included information on Canadian knitting.

Hansen, who is known as a "mitten folklorist," lives in Maine and has spent years travelling, studying, and writing about traditional mittens. She recognizes that the mittens of New England and Atlantic Canada share many aspects of the same North Atlantic knitting culture, which has Western European, Scandinavian, and even Baltic roots.

Janetta Dexter wrote that in Eastern Canada "double knitting" means "knitting with two contrasting colors in an all-over pattern in which the thread not in use is carried along on the wrong side of the work. This gives an extra layer of wool in the finished work making it doubly warm."[22] It does not refer to mittens made in two separate layers of fabric from the cuffs down, a different technique that some writers consider "true" double-knit mittens.

As the authors discovered, establishing the pedigree of a mitten is a dangerous business. Just when a knitting authority attempts to pinpoint some distinctive origins, some contradictory evi-

A bevy of Canadian mittens and gloves

dence turns up. Indeed, some particular snowflake designs are so well known that they seem universal among mitten-wearing peoples. Moreover, many traditional mittens are cross-cultural products. In Labrador, for example, the Moravian missionaries taught Inuit women European patterns that are still knit today, sometimes using the continental method of throwing the yarn with the left hand.

The beguiling names of patterns are as much a part of the oral tradition as are the knitting techniques themselves. Who can resist the charm of patterns that beckon from what seem like simpler times with names like Northern Star, Diamonds and Waves, Fox and Geese, and Mattie Owl's Patch?

Mattie Owl was a native woman who lived in Guysborough County, Nova Scotia. One evening she called on a neighbour:

> *Mattie Owl was wearing a ragged pair of double-knit mittens which had been patched with scraps from other handknits, and the [neighbour's] eye was caught by the double-knit pattern on the patches.*
>
> *She gave Mattie Owl a pair of new double-knit mittens then and there in trade for the ragged pair, and when Mattie Owl left, [she] must have promptly sat down and copied the pattern in new yarn, because her family has knit mittens in that pattern ever since, calling it Mattie Owl's Patch.*[23]

Knitters are among the most resourceful of people and no known force can stop a knitter who covets a new pattern.

Finger Mitts

Hand knitters are born innovators. Over the centuries, they have become admirable mitten technologists, developing ever better shapings and always improving the use of available materials.

Finger mitts are a fine example of this adaptive skill. Really a cross between mittens and gloves, they have separate compartments for both the thumb and index finger. They are excellent to wear when a cold weather task requires fine motor control, especially thumb-finger opposition. The glove, the dressier relative of the finger mitt, is naturally useful for these tasks, but less warm, since fingers separately encased cannot rub together to promote circulation and generate heat.

Finger mitts were sometimes used as shooting mitts because a trigger could be pulled without removing the mitt. As a result, hunters often wore them. They were also worn in wartime when they were an important piece of the serviceman's knitted gear. Wartime patterns had many versions of "gunner's mittens" as they were called. They were also preferred by fishermen who must often bait hooks and tie knots.

In a quite different sphere of life, a rumour in artistic circles has it that members of the Group of Seven had specially designed finger mitts for outdoor painting expeditions. The thumb, forefinger, and index finger were separate while the last two fingers were joined. This made grasping fine brushes much easier.

Finger mitts were usually double-knit in dark and light homespun yarn. Some of the most commonly used motifs were the diamond and the "salt and pepper" pattern. Many pairs were needed in the course of a year, and women were kept constantly busy making them. One Newfoundland woman described her husband's inordinate need for mittens in the words, "They don't do him jig time, because he tears them up."[24]

The development of insulated work gloves has circumscribed the need for hand-knit finger mittens among outdoorsmen, but thousands of pairs continue to be knit for their unique beauty and serviceability. They are a pleasure to make and to wear.

Lobster Mitts

Fishing mittens were often knit oversize deliberately because the action of salt water would cause them to shrink in time. Robin Hansen comments that when a fisherman's mitts got wet, he would sometimes remove them and dry them on the manifold of the engine of his boat. They would naturally shrink while drying. This led some clever knitters to capitalize on the shrinking properties of wool to create a felted mitten, known in the Atlantic provinces as a "lobster mitt." Leaving nothing to chance, parts of the mitten were originally knit up to three times the desired size, then soaked in salt water, plunged into hot soapy water, and dried near a hot stove several times in succession. Each time it would shrink a bit more until finally the knitter had made a thick, tough mitten that would be virtually waterproof under most conditions.

Not every knitter took so deliberate an approach. Many women simply made an oversize mitt and left the shrinking to nature. As one New Brunswick woman remembered,

> *We'd knit them up to maybe 14 inches long. By the end of lobster season they'd fit just right!* [25]

Some of the superstitions that go along with living the dangerous life of a fisherman came to govern knitting as well. Author Evelyn Richardson tells us that, in one part of Nova Scotia, natural cream coloured wool was preferred for mittens that would be worn aboard a boat since grey mittens were regarded as bad luck. The fact is that "white" yarn may be warmer and mats and shrinks more readily to become wind and waterproof.

Other Fishing Mittens

Ingenuity knew no bounds when knitting was pressed into the service of fishing, for fishermen depend on their hands a great deal. One type of mitten covered only the palm of the hand with no more than one inch of covering for the thumb and fingers. This was aptly named a "wrister." These protected men's wrists from being chafed by the edges of their oilskins and from the painful boils that this caused. They are still worn today, some-

times under other mittens. When the outer mitten is pulled off to do fine work, the wrister stays on. They also make a soft, protective layer between the skin and an insulated work glove.

In Newfoundland, where cod fishing was dominant, a similar garment was called a "header's mitt." It was worn when cleaning fish and protected the palm of the hand, which was pressed against the backbone of the fish again and again during endless hours of repetitive work. Moreover, such was the division of labour in cleaning the fish that a different "splitter's mitt" was also knit.

Nippers and Stalls

"Nippers" and "stalls" were about the most abbreviated form of hand covering that a knitter could possibly make. Robin Hansen gives the following description of nippers, which protected the hands when hauling in fishing line.

A Nipper looks like two stuffed tubes of knitting attached together along one side and at

Fleece mittens knit by Dukhobours, 1984.

both ends. They were slipped on, one to a hand, over the palm, and cushioned the hand against the bite of the rope while actually providing more fetch and grip than the hand [itself] can manage on a narrow line.[26]

In days gone by, when hand lining was virtually the only way to fish, nippers were an essential form of protection against rope burns. Today, hydraulic machinery does some of the hard physical work in fishing, and there is less need for hand-made nippers, but fishermen must still take good care of their hands.

Stalls were knitted finger coverings that were worn selectively whenever any particular digit was subjected to chafing and needed protection. A thumb stall, for example, might be worn when cleaning fish to keep the splitter's thumb from wearing out during endless repetitions of the same motion. Many individual stalls could be knit in the time it took to make a pair of mittens, so they were sometimes a sensible alternative for warmer shore work.

Working in salt water with open sores on the hands was terribly painful, so fishermen knew the value of keeping their hands in good condition. It was critical to their livelihood, and the care and ingenuity of knitters made all the difference.

Fleece Mittens

Fleece mittens had bits of carded but unspun wool fibre tucked into them for added warmth. The raw wool was worked in back of the knit stitches, so it was invisible on the outside of the work. When it eventually matted, it provided a very thick, warm lining nearly as warm as sheepskin itself.

There are many different names for fleece mittens. In Newfoundland, the technique for making them was usually known as "thrum" knitting, "thrummed knitting," "drum" knitting or "stuffed" knitting.

Winterhouses, the company that specializes in traditional knitting from the Port-au-port peninsula of Newfoundland, describes the origins of thrum knitting.

Years ago in England, the woollen mills would discard slubs of wool, called "thrums" which knitters would gather and use in their mittens to add extra texture and warmth. This tradition was brought to Newfoundland by the settlers and after being almost forgotten for years, has been revived.[27]

There are many ways to work the fleece into a mitten, governed only by the endless versatility of the hand knitter. In thrum knitting, the fleece is caught at regular intervals when a specific number of stitches and rows has been knit. This spacing keeps the fabric from becoming too tight and cramping the movement of the fingers. Instead of creating an entire thrummed mitten, some knitters simply worked small pockets of thrum knitting for selective padding here and there on the hardest working parts of the mitten.

The traditional art of making fleece mittens is very popular today, and the principle of "waste not, want not" is still heeded in woollen mills. Workers at Briggs & Little in New Brunswick knit dozens of pairs of these mitts in their spare moments, using bits of waste pencil roving from the mill. They call their mittens "fluffies." Thrum knitting is now high art in Newfoundland and has expanded beyond the simple making of mittens. Why should the benefits of warmth be restricted to the hands only? Beautiful thrum knit caps, socks, and vests are wonderfully warm to wear too.

Thrum knitting from Newfoundland

There is no limit to what a knitter's creativity can produce when unleashed on the materials at hand. Canada's folk knitting shows that developing functional and beautiful garments is not the prerogative of professional clothing designers — it has always been an everyday thing with knitters.

The Quest for Warm Feet

While today's beginning knitter will likely debut by making a simple scarf or sweater, in days gone by many young people cut their knitting teeth on a pair of socks. This is remarkable when one considers that a properly fitting and hard-wearing sock is an engineering marvel and that an embellished sock is very nearly a work of art. The pleasures of wearing a good hand-knit sock are so great that happy indeed is one who has a sock knitter for a friend!

Nearly every knitter can remember in great detail the momentous experience of learning "to turn a heel." It seems to be a critical point in a knitter's development, perhaps equal to mastering one of the key elements of the stonemason's art in medieval times. The photographs of yesterday's knitters that survive today usually show women knitting socks while sitting in their rocking chairs, while posing for formal portraits in the parlour, or while snatching a few moments from everyday tasks like drawing water from a well. Sock knitting was the definition of perpetual motion for the Canadian woman.

Socks and Status

Good socks have always been essentials in the Canadian climate, but status conscious colonists like Susanna Moodie also pointed to a well-clad foot as a sign of social superiority. Her description of "an impudent, bare legged Irish servant-girl" underlines her idea of the twin stigma in the new land of being both without hose and Irish. Clearly, in the New World everyone must have socks.

In later times and in a different part of the country, Lucy Maud Montgomery mocked those foolish and vain people with insufficient footwear for Canadian conditions. One stormy night in February 1892, two men took shelter in her Prince Edward Island home. The young and precocious Lucy Maud wrote:

> Uncle John brought them in all covered with snow...they had got upset in a snowdrift behind our barn. I was glad to see James...[but] Mytton was a case! He was a thin little Englishman, dressed as if for a party in light summer clothes and patent leather shoes and he was half frozen. We got them down to the fire and thawed them out.[28]

Yesterday's Footwear

Yesterday's outer footwear was vastly unlike today's miracles of lightweight warmth and required thick socks to be effective. One diarist from Nova Scotia's Annapolis Valley described typical winter wear in the early days of this century as follows:

> The footgear worn in the wintertime by some of the schoolboys is perhaps worth mentioning. They were called "shanks" and were worn when there was plenty of snow. Men sometimes wore them too, generally when they were working in the woods. What are shanks? Well, when a farmer killed a beef animal, the elbow of hide over the hock was cut off and split open on the front side. The hair was left on (an essential feature) and there was only a very little curing of the skin; it was merely scraped and some salt rubbed into it. Then it was made into a shoe-pac. The toe was sewed up, and holes punched for lacing the rest of the way. I tell you, it made a dainty little slipper! They were worn with anywhere from two to four pairs of heavy, gray woolen socks, with a handful or two of straw on the bottom.[29]

Inelegant, perhaps, but convenient and very interesting to posterity.

The Worksock

The earliest socks were sewn from fabric or made from skins. During the fur trade, intrepid voyageurs went about their business barefoot inside their skin boots. This surely could not have been by choice. No amount of misplaced machismo could possibly compensate for the comfort of a well-protected foot.

But a warm, dry foot, undoubtedly one of the prerequisites of civilized life and energetic thought, could be an elusive thing in a northern country. Even in Canada's Arctic communities today, the stylish leather boot and thin nylon stocking mark the southerner, for a time that is. Northerners merely shake their heads...and await the inevitable plunging of the thermometer.

In the country's milder coastal areas, the problem was often one of staying dry. Evelyn Richardson wrote about her life as a lighthouse keeper's wife on a comparatively temperate island off the Nova Scotia mainland.

> Even in the summer we wear more clothes than we would inland. The winds, and especially the fog-breezes, are cool, and a sweater is always welcome. Rubber boots for the wet land demand woollen socks; and the path to the boathouse and the way along the beach

Three Nova Scotia sock knitters

tops is too rough for lighter footwear, even when the weather is dry.[30]

No matter where one lived, there were problems with cold feet. Richardson also struck a sympathetic chord when discussing the nearly universal problem of cold feet among women in bed. "My feet," she said, "are usually numb with the cold when I work about the kitchen, and Morrill is long-suffering as a bedfellow."[31]

One Christmas, a relative sent Evelyn the gift of a hot water bottle at the same time as her husband received a blow-torch. His comment was, "Gee! Doug certainly means me to have comfort this winter. Nights that the hot water bottle won't do the trick, I can apply the blow-torch."[32]

The true solution for cold feet of any kind was, of course, the worksock, that precursor of unisex dressing for warmth. Evelyn put practicality above fashion and shared her secret with us:

My feet haven't been quite so icy since I found a pair or two of the men's long woollen stockings in an outgrown pair of [men's] shoes.... I shiver just to imagine silk stockings and slippers, which I once considered ample for winter house wear.[33]

Sock Reinforcers

Socks wear out more quickly when worn in boots and as soon as nylon yarns appeared on the market, sock knitters seized upon them to reinforce heels. Before nylon, however, ingenuity was needed. The heel of a sock, for example, could be knit with a double thickness. When a heel wore out, some people preferred to cover the hole with a patch of denim or other heavy cloth, and pressed the sock into service once more. Heels could certainly be darned and usually were, and many men who could not knit their own socks knew how to darn them. Some thoughtful women knew that a darned heel could be uncomfortable when worn in a boot, so they used a cloth patch to make their menfolk's lives easier.

Some women also knit "heelless" socks. These were simple tubes of ribbed knitting with one end sewn together for the toe. Men forced into the bachelor life of the bunkhouse particularly liked these. When they wore out in one spot, they could simply be turned back to front, and the hole moved to a less important but likely more visible spot. In case of extreme need, the "toe" could also be moved to the other end.

Women in Atlantic Canada knit "vamps" to combat the problem of wear. Vamps were short socks that extended only as far as the ankle. They could be more quickly replaced than an entire sock. Vamps were pulled on over the standard sock to prevent its heel from playing out so quickly. "Vamp" could also mean a sort of knitted slipper, sometimes with a leather sole sewn to it. One man described the way he relaxed in the evening as "sitting by myself in the kitchen...with my boots off, a pair of woolen vamps hauled over my socks, and with my feet up on the pan of the stove smokin' my pipe."[34]

Socks of a Sourdough

During the Klondike Gold Rush, which began in 1896, prospectors were advised to have a minimum of twelve pairs of woollen socks among their gear, enough to last one year on the trail. The Hudson Bay Company, hoping to gain a large part of the outfitting business, provided a ready-made kit for one miner for one year for between $190 and $220. In addition to provisions, mining equipment, and general clothing requirements, the outfit included the following items:

Gloves, skin	1 pair
Gloves, wool	1 pair
Mitts, leather	1 pair
Mitts, wool	1 pair
Socks, wool	12 pairs
Sweaters, wool	2 only
Underwear, wool	3 suits
Socks, long Arctic	2 pairs[35]

The recommendation of twelve pairs of socks, one for each month of the year, gives rise to speculation about the frequency of washing among the men who moiled for gold. Perhaps, the life span of a sourdough's worksock was thought to be simply one month of constant hard wear, with no changes planned.

Compare the difference in sock requirements and standards when a good wife was in charge of the supply. Evelyn Richardson made these comments about her family's socks:

The men...must have innumerable sweaters and socks. It is not unusual for me to have a dozen pairs of socks for them in the weekly wash, most of them with their heels completely chewed out from walking in their rubber boots. I knit their sweaters and socks out of white and grey yarn from the woollen mill

Worksocks hang to dry while dinner is cooked in a logging camp.

at Barrington. This yarn is not soft or fine, but it wears exceptionally well, and garments knit from it can be laundered weekly in the washer with as little fuss as any cotton piece. The men like their socks long enough to turn down below the knees of their breeches, so that means plenty of knitting in each leg. I never catch up on my knitting and it seems I always have a sock, or sweater, or mitten in the making for "pick-up" work.[36]

Socks for Woodsmen

What were the "long Arctic Socks" that were recommended by the Hudson's Bay Company? Perhaps they resembled what some women on the South Shore of Newfoundland called "buskins." Buskins were a sort of legging that were worn over boots. They extended up almost to the knee on the outside of the pants to keep out the snow. They were sometimes worn by men when they went into the bush to cut fire wood. Or perhaps they were

like the long oversocks knit by many women across Canada. One described these as, "so big they looked like stovepipes when finished."[37] They had both a ribbed top and a drawstring to hold them up.

Loggers certainly had a great demand for socks and still do today. Photographs of life in the logging camps and shanties of yesterday often show thick worksocks hanging up to dry — or at least to smoke — near the camp stove. They often look rather ragged and in need of a good darn.

Tam O'Shanters and Toques

In cold weather, most body heat escapes through the top of the head, not through the hands or feet. In a northern country, mitts and socks are the stuff of everyday wear, but a hat is a garment that makes a statement. This is true today, and it was even more obvious in the heavy hat-wearing annals of history when style of headcover positively indicated social station. In a medieval painting, for example, each person may wear a different type of hat. In photographs of Canadian crowd scenes from years ago, every single person wears a hat, including children.

Some hats traditionally worn in Canada have roots in medieval Europe. The beret, for example, is a traditional French knitted cap. They were originally made several sizes too big and fulled in much the same way as lobster mitts. The controlled shrinkage produced a dense woollen fabric that looked like cloth, and only the very knowledgeable could detect their knitted origins. Genuine wool berets are still made by this method in France today. Many are worn by their elite Alpine troops.

The brimmed Newfoundland "salt and pepper" cap is similar in shape to the English knitted "porkpie" hat, which was also fulled. The knitted felt fabric was sometimes cut to make a decorative brim. The method of knitting caps of this type has been well analysed, since some very old examples are kept in English museums.

Tam o'shanters were worn by members of the Orillia Hockey Club, 1895.

Jacques Plante wearing a hand-knit toque.

Perhaps because Scottish colonists were so numerous here, the tam o'shanter became one of Canada's most popular knitted hats. In her history of Scottish knitting, Helen Bennett tells us that the first professional knitters in Scotland were bonnetmakers and that by 1496 the bonnetmakers of Dundee were sufficiently numerous to form a trade guild. The hats that they made were much like tam o'shanters as we know them. Like the French beret, they were fulled and had the appearance of finely woven cloth. It was not until about 1870 that knitting machines operated by factory workers began to replace the old hand-knit caps of Scotland, and this was long after they had left their imprint on Canadian knitters.

The tam o'shanter was the all-purpose sporting cap here at the turn of the century. They were even worn by community hockey teams. Today's backyard hockey players can scarcely be persuaded to wear any hat at all, and when they do, they usually don a toque. Jacques Plante, longtime goaltender for the Montreal Canadiens hockey team, knit his own and set quite a fashion for them.

The toque must surely be the quintessential Canadian hat. An abbreviated version of the stocking cap, toques are worn by popular figures from hockey players to Bonhomme Carnaval. They are enshrined in the mythology of life in the True North Strong and Free. The red stocking cap of Bonhomme Carnaval, mascot of the Quebec Winter Carnival, is a descendant of the hats worn by the patriots in the French Revolution — the side who managed to keep their heads.

"Habitant Driving a Sleigh/habitant conduisant un traîneau," Cornelius Krieghoff, 1815–1872

Bonhomme Carnaval greets distinguished visitors wearing his famous stocking cap.

In Canada, the voyageurs often wore toques when they were not wearing tall beaver hats or other colourful headwear. They loved to make a dashing personal fashion statement. The paintings of Cornelius Krieghoff show groups of lusty *habitants* having fun in their jaunty toques. If people are what they wear, the rakishness of their caps probably gave the voyageurs their devil-may-care attitude.

Working Sweaters

Traditionally, the sweater was a man's working garment. Women wore shawls, nightingales, shoulderettes, and woollen vests to keep the upper body warm. It was not until the twentieth century that sweaters became the unisex garment and knitters' *tour de force* that we know so well today. Some say that Coco Chanel was the first to popularize sweater dressing for women in the early decades of this century and that she modelled her first designs on the knits worn by British men.

The Canadian man's working sweater is directly descended from British jerseys and guernseys, or "ganseys" as they were sometimes called. Both have the same circular construction and simple shaping. On both sides of the Atlantic, they were a practical working outfit that provided excellent freedom of movement and could be layered with other garments. Layers could be stripped off when the activity heated up.

Evelyn Richardson described a typical Canadian duck hunting uniform in this way:

Three sweaters, or two sweaters and a windbreaker are none too many, and these are topped by an oilskin or rubber jacket "to break the wind." If there is snow down an old white sweater goes outside this so it doesn't show against the whitened beach. I knit a special shawl collar for each of Morrill's gunning sweaters, so this comes well up about his neck to prevent chafing by the oilskin collar, and stops the wind from blowing down the back of his neck when he is prone.[38]

Woodsmen also found sweaters ideal and many photographs show loggers wearing them in the lumber camps. They usually wore a neckerchief as well, possibly to prevent chafing but more likely to catch the perspiration before it rolled down their necks into their sweaters. It was undoubtedly much easier to wash a neckerchief than a sweater. Perhaps it was their natural absorbency that caused plain-speaking Canadians to name them "sweaters" instead of "jumpers."

The fisherman's sweater was commonly worn in Canada too and was styled much like its British counterpart. But efforts to document a link between the stitch patterns of Canada and the rich stitch patterns of Britain are doomed to failure. Photographs of garments past do not help. Most pictures of Canadian fishermen were taken ashore in summer weather, and the subjects are usually wearing shirt sleeves. Those sweaters that are visible seem to be plainly knit or enlivened only by a simple stripe of contrasting yarn.

Along with the essentials of the garment, some British sweater vocabulary crossed the Atlantic with the settlers. In Newfoundland, where many linguistic Anglicisms survive, the use of the term "gansey," or even "garnsey" has been documented. The *Dictionary of Newfoundland English* defines it as "a heavy, closely-knit pullover sweater worn by fishermen and sealers." Another writer summed up its essential design features in the words "a heavy woolen knitted man's garment with no opening back or front, pulled on over the head and reaching just below the waist."[39]

In 1933, William Howe Greene described the dress of the intrepid Newfoundland seal hunter. The word "jumper" here means a canvas jacket worn as outerwear.

Then with thick woollen garnseys, oilskins, sou'westers, and stout canvas jumpers, the outfit is complete and the men are ready — and more than willing too.[40]

Artist David Blackwood has given us many haunting and powerful images of the sealers of yesterday. We are also indebted to him for a story about a sealer's sweater that was put to sterner uses.

The annual seal hunt off the coast of Newfoundland was a male rite of passage, as well as a much needed economic measure. In 1914, when he was just seventeen years of age, young Albert John Winsor set off for the hunt. He went contrary to his mother's wishes, as is often the way of young men, and signed on with the *S.S. Newfoundland* without his parents' consent. When his father heard the news, he said to his wife, "Mary, I...the only thing I can see is for me to go with him, I

wouldn't trust him there alone. I know what the seal fishery's like."[41]

So the two went together. One night soon after their departure a terrible storm caught the sealers unprepared and stranded them on the ice with great loss of life. Asleep at home the mother had a disturbing dream. As she remembered it, she was awakened about midnight by a moonbeam that shone in through her window. It shone past her bed and on her husband and son.

"...they were so close you could see the double stitching that I put on their canvas jackets. They were both kneeling in an attitude of prayer. I looked at their faces and they were so peaceful and happy looking. And it was just for a few seconds, and they disappeared."[42]

Blackwood tells us that both father and son perished in the disaster. When they found young Albert John, he was snuggled under his father's sweater and canvas jacket — and that's where he died. The two of them were frozen together in death.

The mother's heart, though terribly grieved, must have found a measure of solace in that image.

The Canadian working sweater never reached the heights of patterned beauty that its British counterpart did. With centuries of development behind it, the British guernsey remained a working garment but became a display case for the talent and skill of some of the most able knitters the world has ever known. The Canadian sweater remained plain and useful and its written history is like the garment itself — short and simple.

Wartime Knitting in Canada

The Call to Knit

Most knitters have a well-developed sense of generosity that comes from doing so much unselfish knitting for others. In fact, personal knitting has probably accounted for very little of all the work that has been done throughout history. Nothing has ever stimulated this sense of altruism more than wartime knitting. Doing something to make a loved one look more beautiful is an inspiration, but making a pair of seaboot stockings for a young sailor standing a lonely watch on the deck of a supply ship must have seemed truly urgent and worthwhile.

As in other parts of the world, Canadians were spurred on to truly Herculean efforts of wartime knitting. Pulling together is the rule in wartime, and the skills of all were made to count regardless of age, sex, or social standing. Men, women, and children in Canada knit their way through two world wars and the Korean Conflict. Many of today's best knitters acquired their basic skills in wartime, when children in Canadian schools took on major knitting challenges.

The British royal family has always set an example when it comes to clothing servicemen in wartime. Queen Victoria may have been the first. She was known to have made eight scarves, four for British soldiers and four to be given to the four most distinguished private soldiers serving in colonial regiments during the Boer War (1899–1902): Private Duprayer, New South Wales; Private Coutts, New Zealand; Trooper Chadwick, Cape Colony; and Private Thompson, Canada.

Private Richard Roland Thompson served as a medical orderly. On one occasion, he lay exposed to enemy fire for over seven hours with his thumb and fingers pressed against a wounded comrade's shattered jugular vein.

The Queen Victoria Scarf, presented to a Canadian soldier for bravery, proved to be crocheted.

Alas for knitters, when the scarf made for Private Thompson was recently examined in the Canadian War Museum in Ottawa, it proved to be crocheted. Queen Victoria was a knitter, but her eyesight weakened in later years and crochet became easier to do. Nevertheless, an example of patriotic needlework had been begun by the royals. During World War II, the present Queen Mother and the princesses were photographed knitting for the war effort, and knitting parties were frequently held in Buckingham Palace.

Knitting was considered very critical indeed, and not simply to provide moral support for the fighting forces. A warm army was an effective army. "Men fight, and conquer, in WOOL" was the slogan.

Canadians knit for active soldiers, airmen, sailors, merchant seamen, and servicewomen. We knit for the sick and wounded, for convalescents, and for prisoners of war. We knit for children in Britain and Europe and for refugees from war-torn countries. And while all this was going on, we continued to knit for ourselves and for our families.

Much private knitting was done for local boys and for individual family members overseas, but the large-scale mobilization of Canadian knitters in wartime was and continues to be unprecedented in our history.

During World War I, the Canadian Red Cross Society distributed yarn and patterns, ensured quality control, and collected finished goods. It also played a major role in distributing garments overseas. Many other organizations, including ladies' auxiliaries and church groups, played a significant part, particularly as producers of knitted items. Chapters of the Imperial Order of the Daughters of the Empire alone knit and sewed more than two million items during World War I. Knitting was not just for adults. Young people belonging to the Junior Home Reserves, the Canadian Girl Guides, the Junior Red Cross, and other youth organizations joined them as producers.

The administrative work behind the knitting effort was complex and time-consuming, but it must have given many knitters some rather unexpected high-level administrative experience and a true sense of the value of their work outside the home environment.

Some branches of the service organized the knitting effort on behalf of their own forces. In this way, they could specify exactly what was wanted and minimize distribution time. The Navy League of Canada was a case in point. During World War II, the Navy League led the knitting effort for the Canadian Navy and Merchant Navy. Founded in

1918, the Navy League is still active today as a volunteer organization. It prepared, distributed, and translated its own pattern books; supplied the yarn; and distributed the finished goods to men in need.

The introduction to one of its pattern books, *Knit! Knit! Knit! for the Navy and Merchant Navy*, describes the magnitude of its mission.

> *The Navy League of Canada, Ontario Division, has undertaken a huge task in the matter of supplying knitted garments, sweaters, caps, scarfs, wristlets, and other needed supplies and comforts for Canadian Seamen who enter the ports of Canada on the Atlantic and Pacific Coasts.*
>
> *We have more than 30,000 sailors in the Royal Canadian Navy, in addition to the many thousands of Merchant Seamen serving on Canadian ships.*
>
> *It is the desire of the Navy League to secure the cooperation of individuals and organizations interested in the welfare of these men and the service they are rendering in protecting the interests of Canadian citizens.*

Members of the I.O.D.E., the Red Cross, the United Church of Canada, and other organizations were represented on the Navy League National Council. It did the actual work of distributing the wool and collecting the finished garments.

A "ditty bag" was the name given to the navy blue canvas bags that were stuffed with knitted goods, cigarettes, candies, toiletries, and other treats and distributed to seamen. The ditty bag programme was launched in earnest in 1940, when the Council of the Navy League prepared a list of suggested articles for the bag. As the war advanced, this list changed in response to sailor's comments, but warm woollens remained at the heart of it.

Knitters were advised that the list could be modified as they saw fit; and many sailors preferred to be surprised by the contents of their bag rather than get the same things each time. Knitters were encouraged to enclose friendly letters that would provide a personal morale boosting link between themselves and the sailors.

The demand for ditty bags increased. Records show that at least 100,000 bags were distributed in 1942, of which 20,000 were supplied by the I.O.D.E., 30,000 by the Red Cross, and the remainder by other volunteer organizations. An extensive advertising programme requesting ditty bag donations was initiated. Messages on milk

bottles seemed a good way to get the word out. The city of Hamilton, Ontario, for example, arranged to have all milk bottle caps carry the message "Fill a Ditty Bag for a Sailor Now!" Large window display cards were exhibited by Loblaws, Tamblyn Drugs, and Owl and United Cigar stores. It would have been difficult indeed for an able-bodied knitter to ignore these appeals.

Toward the end of the war, wool had grown very expensive and no one could afford the yarn to knit large items like sweaters for every sailor. Eventually the number of woollen items in the ditty bag was slimmed down to socks alone and the size of the bag was also reduced. As well, another kind of bag called the "survivor's bundle" began to be distributed. This ominous name gives a sobering indication of developments in the war at sea in later years. It was a bare-bones ditty bag without the amusements and treats, but it included some large clothing items such as a suit of underwear, a knitted turtle-neck sweater, and a pair of socks.

Did sailors appreciate their ditty bags? Indeed they did. The Navy League received 6,500 letters of thanks from seamen in one year alone. It had the excellent idea of publishing extracts from these letters in its pattern books to complete the personal link between sailor and knitter. The letters brought to mind the risks of life on board ship in wartime and the sailors' need to communicate with everyday people doing everyday things on shore. It is also easy to forget how terribly young most of them were.

> *...many thanks for your Christmas presents. I'm a Norwegian sailor and very glad for all the things you have put in the bag. We are 30 men on board our ship and they all got a bag with presents from Toronto. That's good of you people, so far away, to think of us sailors...*

> *...just a note of sincere thanks for the suit [of underwear] and woollens I received from your Navy League. The suit was one thing I was in need of at the time, having lost everything at sea. The sweater and socks fit me fine and are very comfortable...*

> *...I am an apprentice aboard this ship and I am seventeen, only being at sea for one year running to Montreal and Saint John all the time. In my short time at sea I have lost two ships, and we hope that will be all...*

No knitter ever needed any greater encouragement to knit.

Service Woollies

The term "service woollies" was coined by Patons & Baldwins in its pattern books and came to stand for all wartime garments. Canadians took on the task of knitting any necessary thing that could be made out of yarn, from wristlets to cotton wash cloths. Every serviceman needed warm everyday socks and mitts, but a great many specialty items were made, too, and not wanting raggle taggle armed forces, garments were usually made to match a regulation uniform.

The greatest need was for socks, and not just any haphazardly made sock would do. The length was stipulated, usually eleven inches for the finished foot. During World War I, the approved patterns specified that a coloured stripe be knit at the top of the sock. The colour could not be red, however, because red dye was not fast and could infect a wound in the muddy trenches of France and Belgium.

A remarkable programme of knitter education was doubtless part of the war effort, and the motivation to learn was never stronger. Patterns specified that the toe of a sock must be grafted together to make a smooth join and gave explicit instructions for doing this — any type of seam became uncomfortable after a few hundred yards on a marching foot.

Sometimes, there were options. One pattern book offered the knitter "your choice of single or double heel, round or flat toe," and some knitters must have been delighted to extend their technical and cultural horizons to a pair of "heavy socks with French heel and Kitchener toe." "Make a wearable sock!" another book urged, and many an old knitter must have learned a new trick or improved upon a known one, recognizing that he or she wanted to be part of the solution, not part of the problem.

Sea boot stockings were a specialty item for the naval forces in World War II. These were long, over the knee socks with a ribbed cuff that could be folded down. The standard length was twenty-six inches. They were coarsely knit, requiring about fourteen ounces of "wheeling wool." Sea boot stockings were in great demand in the Merchant Navy and pattern books exhorted knitters with the words, "the Merchant Navy is Britain's life-line. You play an important part when you knit for these men."

In 1943, navy sock-knitting technology took a great leap forward. Dr. Charles Best, co-discoverer of insulin, was a navy man and a medical advisor to the Navy League. With other prominent naval associates, he focussed his considerable abilities on designing a sock that would prevent "immersion foot." (Many limbs of shipwrecked sailors were lost because lengthy exposure to wet conditions caused a breakdown in blood circulation and resulted in gangrene. This was invariably followed by amputation.)

The remedy was the "medicated stocking," which consisted of a "specially spiral knit woollen garment which, when completed, was impregnated by special process with a petrolatum solution."[43] The final product was packed by pairs in a treated waterproof container. The entire project was intriguing and ingenious. We do not know what these stockings looked like, but Navy League minutes report that "the ready response by our ladies to knit these very important socks was most encouraging and gratifying." Six thousand pairs were made.

Wartime mitts and gloves were designed for many special purposes, ranging from "naval artillery" (also called "gunnery") mitts to the sobering "minesweepers'" mitts. Many of Canada's coastal knitters must have found it easy to fill their personal quota of gunnery mitts because these were identical to the familiar finger mitts made for fishermen.

Shaped like traditional lobster mittens, parts of minesweepers' mitts were actually crocheted, using wool and a tough cotton twine for extra strength. Waterproof material was basted to them in certain places. And the maker was urged to work them loosely to allow for shrinkage.

"Rifle" mitts lacked thumb and forefinger compartments for the obvious reason. "Two-way" mitts had a slot near the palm so that fingers could be released for brief periods and then quickly reinserted. "Observers' gloves" were totally fingerless. "Gloves are urgently needed overseas," the knitter was told. All of these hand coverings allowed precision work to be done without removing the entire mitten and having to keep track of its whereabouts in the midst of a life and death struggle.

The "merchant navy pullover" was a traditional guernsey with a thick turtle-neck. There were many calls for these and their usefulness could not be over-estimated. The North Atlantic is a grim place in winter in peacetime; in wartime, it must have been quite terrifying.

The knitted vest was in great demand in all branches of the service, and there were many similar patterns for these. Keeping the neck warm must have been a major problem, judging by the many garments knit for this purpose. The Air Force, for example, preferred its sleeveless vests to have a turtle-neck. The "tuck-in," a form of turtle-

Living and working aboard a naval ship in wartime was a challenge that required warm clothes.

neck dickie was very versatile and much needed. Pattern books show these worn slipped inside the neck of a uniform.

Many scarves were also needed, and the most inexpert knitters were urged to knit plain scarves. There must surely have been a great many of these made so that virtual non-knitters could at least save face in public. Highest priority, however, was given to thickly ribbed scarves done in an insulating brioche stitch or to true double-knit scarves. Knitters did not waste much yarn or time on decorative fringes.

By far, the greatest range of designs was for the hats worn by the different branches of the service. The simplest was the "seaman's cap," a traditional cuffed watch cap like those worn by merchant sailors today. The "aero cap" was a watch cap with ear flaps that joined under the chin. Many Air Force missions must have been terribly cold as

well as morally chilling. The "steel helmet cap" was a close-fitting garter stitch cap with a chin strap that fit snugly under an army helmet. It kept a soldier warm and prevented chafing at the same time.

All services wore the balaclava helmet. The "Quebec helmet," the "1940 helmet," and the "Admiral Beatty helmet" are all the same basic shape. The difference is in the style and size of the face openings.

Women's Service Woollies

Not all wartime knitting was destined for men. Some pattern books provided for warm "comforts" for the women of the services. One book reminded knitters that military women were part of the war effort, too.

When you see your friends in uniform these days, it must pop right into your minds that there are gifts of knitted garments they would welcome...and don't forget to tuck several pairs of socks in your gift box.

The most common patterns were for pullovers and cardigans. These were usually multi-purpose, and they were thoughtfully named "utility or service" sweaters so that the woman in uniform could also feel free to wear her well-made sweaters with civilian clothes. One pattern caption recalls the realities of war. "This easy-to-wear, easy-to-knit cardigan," it reads, "has a three-fold use. Make it for friends in the Services, for bomb victims and for general work-o-day wear." On another sweater pattern, the knitter is given the option to "trim it with leather buttons for the Forces, pearl for yourself."

Scarves and gloves were also made, sometimes by making simple adjustments to men's patterns. "Applique leather patches on the palms and fingers of gloves for driving," one book suggests, underlining the new regard for women's work in wartime. Patterns for long stockings and knitted underwear remind us that supplies of prewar lingerie must have dwindled quickly indeed, and many women must have tried to save "one good pair" for dress up.

Hospital Comforts

It is hard for the able-bodied fashion conscious knitter of today to imagine the number and variety of things that were knit for the sick, the wounded, and the convalescent in wartime. The very names of some of these "hospital comforts," as they were called, send a chill down the spine — head bandage covers, body belts, and amputation covers. But surely if anyone needed the comfort that hand-knit garments could provide, it was the hospitalized. This continues to be true and is probably the reason why these wartime patterns are still used for invalids today.

Perhaps because of their sobering purpose, many hospital comforts were made with special thoughtfulness. The "man's convalescent jacket," for example, looked like a normal knitted pullover from the front. The back, however, extended downward only to the shoulder blades, where it was finished off by a thin band of ribbing for firmness. There was no bulk to wrinkle up under the back of a person who must spend much time lying in bed.

Tubular "heelless bed socks" were ideal for feet that would never wear them inside shoes. The "head bandage cover" was surely made to lessen the visual impact on visitors, rather than to satisfy a specific medical purpose. A knitted shoulder wrap was always useful for people whose temperature control might have been disturbed by infection or shock. The perfectly tapered amputation covers were cleverly shaped with a ribbed band and a gently curved tip. They came in two sizes, one for legs and one for arms.

Fanning the Wartime Knitting Flame: Pattern Books

Most pattern books were published in the early years of the war. As time passed and the wartime economy became more firmly established, paper became scarce and of poor quality. The pattern books published during the war that have survived are more fragile than those published before the war began. There was little need for variety and knitters must have memorized the best patterns very quickly. The competitive market for commercial knitting patterns died.

The pattern books that have survived are real treasures. Patons & Baldwins co-published several versions of *Service Woollies For Air, Land and Sea by Beehive* in Britain and in Canada. Hands across the water fought the same war with the same patterns. Beehive patterns, however, were usually sized, whereas many wartime patterns were written for an average figure with little adjustment possible. Considering the possible variations among knitters, some wartime garments must have fit rather oddly indeed. Patons & Baldwins' patterns for the knitting of "hospital comforts" were a strong reminder that war was not very glorious at all.

Because of wartime paper shortages, Lux knitting books were not published between 1944 and 1951. The popular Lux "4-in-one" pattern series, published up to 1944, contained separate sections for women, men, children, and babies. Even in 1941, with the war well advanced, these books still contained many attractive and stylish patterns, including non-military patterns for men's clothing. They called for a wide variety of brand name yarns in exotic colours. Women were urged to try "pale lavender, rich burgundy, and claret red," and to "discover their own personal colour personality." This seems to indicate that until the war intensified and prewar inventories of commodities were exhausted, a normal family life and business as usual were possible for Canadians. As time passed, there were fewer and fewer patterns for attractive clothing and no civilian patterns for

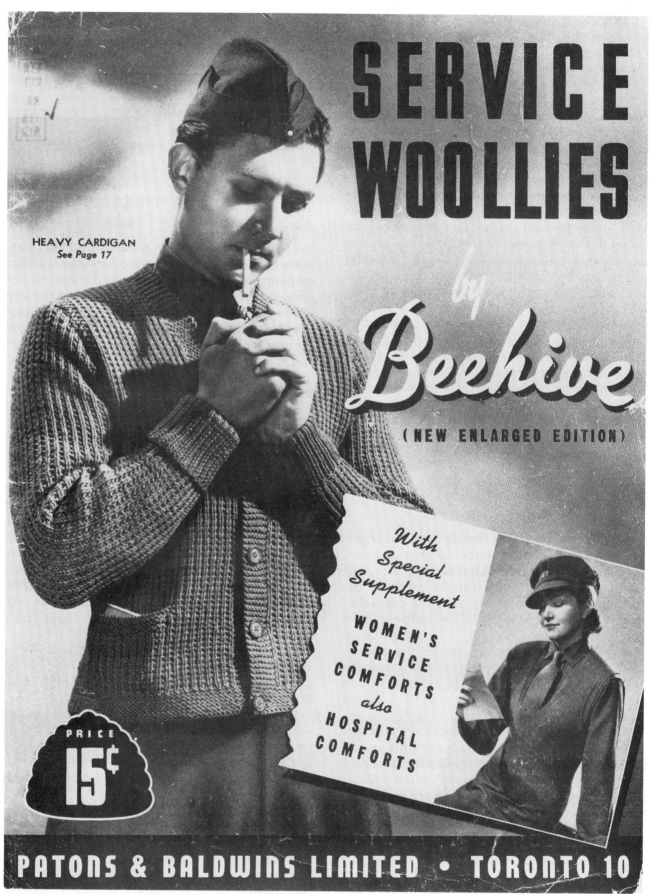

A popular wartime pattern book

men. The ladies' patterns that did appear related hand knitting to economy to an extent that would shock today's marketers.

Virtuoso knitting was put aside for the duration. Plain knitting, in quantity, was the rule. Decorative stitch patterns and special textures were seldom important for service woollies. Almost every garment was made in stocking stitch with ribbed accents — child's play for the expert knitter. Unnecessary ornamentation wasted both time and yarn, and achieving a good, regulation garment shape was all that counted. Patterns were written with this in mind. One knitting book bore the endorsement "Exclusive Service Garments approved by the Canadian Red Cross and the Imperial Order Daughters of the Empire."

Wartime knitting had its puzzling side for the willing novice.

Wartime yarn colours were also restricted. They were not inspiring. A Lux pattern book reminded knitters that the wool chosen should match the uniform, "khaki for the Army, navy blue or black for the Navy, and air force blue for the Air Force

except for officers; they wear black socks." Seamen were permitted to wear grey socks at sea. In every sphere, creativity took a back seat to uniformity and productivity during World War II.

To mitigate some of the undeniable boredom of the repetitive knitting of utilitarian garments that used hard-wearing but unexciting yarns, pattern producers found ways of encouraging knitters' interest. One way was to include plenty of pictures of handsome, smiling servicemen and dedicated nurses doing their duty for their country. The other way was to remind knitters of the gravity of their work.

The Navy League saw to it that knitters knew exactly who they were working for and what their work was worth. One of its pattern books contained a poem. This book would probably have laid open in front of the knitter's eyes until the garment had been completed and/or the pattern and the poem memorized.

> We praise the lads of the Air Force,
> And the Tars of the Navy too,
> We never forget the Army,
> Nor the Anti-Air Craft crew;
> We think of the factory workers,
> And the women in uniform,
> We honour the Red Cross Nurses,
> Who weather many a storm.
> But there's a throng of sailors,
> Who sail the seven seas,
> Braving the submarine's missile,
> And the danger of wave and breeze;
> They do their duty faithfully,
> On many a foreign scene,
> So we doff our caps to the plucky chaps,
> In the Mercantile Marine.[44]

Looking Good on a Budget: The Civilian Side of Wartime Knitting

Despite the horror and waste of war, there was another, more cheerful side to it all. For young, single people, social opportunities were unprecedented, and many a wartime romance led to marriage and postwar babies. Keeping up the morale of servicemen was thought to be nearly as important a patriotic duty as knitting for them, and young women cheerfully obliged. Away from home and with money in their pockets, possibly for the first time, nothing could stop young people from dressing up and going out. Nothing ever has. The knitting pattern people were quick to observe this and to help meet the need for nice looking clothes in the midst of shortages of just about everything.

Accessory dressing became a skill. "Work this smart cable stitch scarf in two colours to dress up last year's coat," one pattern book urges. Explicit instructions on how to unpick knitted garments and prepare the wool for re-knitting also give an indication of wartime exigencies. Such advice today would surely spell doom to our cyclical fashion industry.

Most civilian patterns in these early wartime books were aimed at single girls. The young married woman whose husband was likely far from home was presumed to be already on the shelf and involved in her life of duty. Her selfless alternatives seemed to be knitting for the home and of course, for her children.

Afghan patterns became popular during the early years of the war because they could be made from scraps of yarn. "It takes only twelve yards of wool to make each hexagon," the reader is advised in one pattern. Such limiting factors seriously constrained the exercise of personal taste and selection in a cheerless time of shortages and re-cycling. But the resilient knitting spirit was not quenched by the rigours of wartime. Knitters simply got better at turning inferior straw into gold.

The young wife might also make herself a bedjacket. The number and variety of bedjacket patterns that began to appear foreshadowed the coming of the third, great mass-knitting phenomenon in Canadian history — the postwar baby boom.

Spats, Sacques, and Soakers: The Changing Infant Layette

Many immigrants came to Canada for the purpose of making a better life for their children. Once here, the practical problems of raising and supporting them became only too clear. In *Roughing It in the Bush*, Susanna Moodie summarized this paradox of fertility in the new land in the reported conversation of two pioneers:

"Well, how are you, Mr. S——?" cried the farmer..."Toiling in the bush still, eh?"

"Just in the same place."

"And the wife and children?"

"Hearty. Some half-dozen have been added to the flock since you were our way."

"So much the better — so much the better. The more the merrier, Mr. S——; children are riches in this country."

"I know not how that may be; I find it hard to clothe and feed mine."[45]

This same sentiment is not unknown today.

Knitting for Colonial Babies

The Workwoman's Guide, dating from 1840, is an early instruction book that was much used in Canada and is roughly contemporary with Susanna Moodie's time. It provides us with a fascinating glimpse into early knitting patterns for infants.

The newborn circulatory system being rather unreliable, the first priority was warm feet. These were covered with "socks," "slippers," or "boots," which came to be called "bootees." Every Canadian from the highest to the lowest station in the land has no doubt worn this most famous item of infant footwear — and has probably been photographed wearing them too.

The adventurous nineteenth century knitter might also have tried a pair of "little night boots," made by knitting "a piece of six nails long, and a nail and a half or more deep." We may assume that this refers to the human finger nail as a unit of measurement, not to a piece of hardware.

The Workwoman's Guide has patterns for caps, bonnets, and mittens. A soft, lacy shawl appropriately called a "zephyr" was also part of the ensemble for the tiny one. The interesting thing is that behind the intriguing terminology of yesterday we find the basic infant layette as we know it today: bonnet, bootees, mittens, and shawl. All that is missing is the jacket or sweater.

The Layette Takes Shape

Later knitting books show that the jacket had certainly appeared by the early decades of this century, when sweater dressing for adults also became popular.

Some new items were added to the layette as well. The "infant's sacque," a long tubular sleeping bag, identical to the later "bunting bag," kept baby warm while presumably adding an elegant

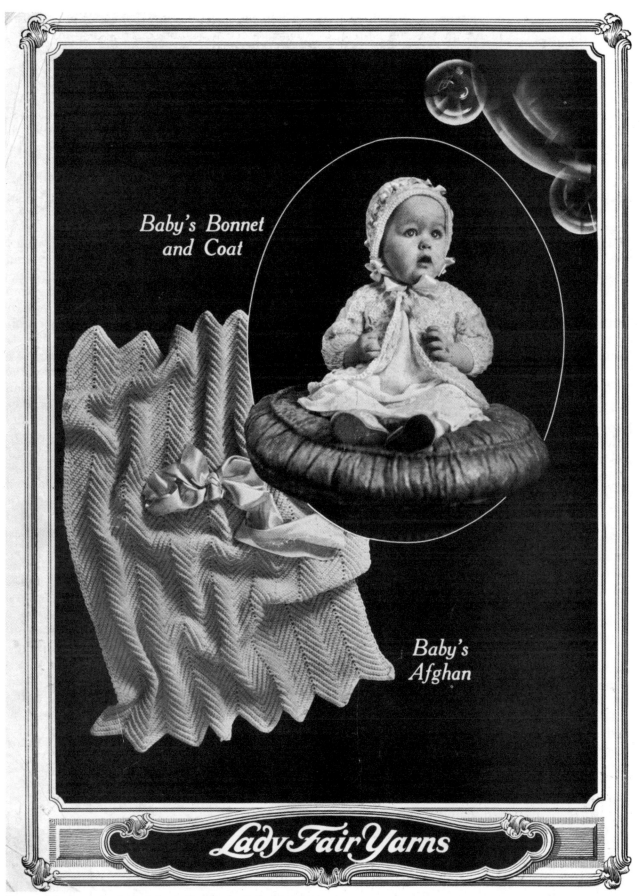

Baby's Bonnet
and Coat

Baby's
Afghan

Lady Fair Yarns

The models for yesterday's baby knits may be today's corporate executives.

French touch to the wardrobe. The "infant's night-ingale," a tiny replica of a lady's garter stitch shawl with cuffs to keep it attached to the hands, kept a baby's back extra warm. The "baby's body belt," an early introduction to the layering principle in infant dressing, must have done much the same.

A lot of thought went into some items of the layette in times past. The "infant's shoulderette" was a neatly crafted miniature shawl that went around baby's shoulders and then buttoned or tied at the waist. Learning to sit up or to enjoy life in the playpen could be a drafty experience in some of the houses in which Canadians grew up.

Perhaps most clever of all was the "baby's-all-in-one," a tiny sweater with decorative thumbless mittens knit downward from the sleeves. This prevented accidental scratchings by sharp finger nails but also reminds us that thumb sucking was one of the sterner prohibitions of past times. Many young mothers measured their worth by victory in the thumb sucking battle.

Knitting for Baby's Bottom

Perhaps the most progressive item to appear in the layette was a covering for baby's bottom known as a "pilch" or "pilch drawers." The T. Eaton Company's *Lady Fair Book of Children's Wear*, published in 1927, provides a pattern which shows them to be a basic three-corner diaper shape with a neat drawstring waist and a button for fastening the bottom flap to the waist. In short, the baby's pilch was a functional antecedent of the "soaker," which was in turn the forerunner of plastic pants. Knitting for baby's bottom had begun.

Soakers were universally worn and most of today's Canadian adults wore hand-knit soakers made by conscientious mothers, which were handed down from child to child for a great many were needed. Patons & Baldwins produced a shrink resistant wool especially for soakers. One ball of "Beehive Soaker Yarn" was all that was needed to make one pair and the instructions were printed on the reverse of the ball band. As late as 1961, *The Canadian Mother and Child*, that fount of all wisdom and reassurance for fearful parents, was still recommending them. Not wishing to further tax harassed mothers, they did not insist too strongly:

There are on the market plastic-lined panties which are easier on the skin and just as effective [as rubber panties]. As long as you change diapers frequently enough, there is no harm in his wearing protective panties for special occasions, but baby should never be put to sleep in them either during the day or at night. Knitted woolen "soakers" are sometimes very useful.[46]

The soaker is a concept that today's mothers find hard to credit. It is easy to understand the logic behind putting a waterproof layer between baby and the rest of the world, but adding a woollen layer, also requiring frequent washing, seems self-defeating.

In the pre-synthetic era there was no choice; wool was the only fibre available. But the reasoning behind soakers is still sound today. Wool is tremendously absorbent and tends to stay comparatively warm when wet. Garments are much more easily washed today and wools are completely shrink resistent so perhaps we may see the return of the soaker in our own environmentally conscious times.

The question of washability never occurred in early baby books. There were no laundry short-cuts and no alternative fibres until very recent times so babies were always dressed in the finest of wools. Mothers went out of their way to find two-ply fingering yarn rather than four-ply yarn for baby clothes. Knitting with these fine yarns is very nearly unthinkable today when most people want the work to "go quickly" and are less expert launderers. Elizabeth Zimmermann, the great Anglo-American knitter, describes the affinity between babies and wool in glowing terms:

Although babies rarely, if ever, express their pleasure at being dressed in wool, it is surely manifest when you dote on a small plump person soundly and contentedly asleep, swaddled in woollen sweater, woollen leggings, and a soft wool bonnet, snugly tucked under a fine warm woolblanket...if there is one fact on which all grandmothers agree, it is that no daughter-in-law knows how to wash wool.[47]

That in a nutshell is the position of wool in infant knitting today.

Togs for Toddlers

By the time baby learned to walk, an entire new wardrobe was required and toddlers had many options open to them. By 1927, a doting mother could knit a one piece suit of "rompers" for her darling boy if she had a mere "4 balls of white Lady Fair Fingering and 1 set of No. 10 needles."

Knitted dresses were popular items for little girls.

Little girls wore fine lace dresses that were absolute marvels of the knitter's art. Entire snowsuits were knit for winter and brief sun-suits for summer. Hand-made snowsuits were the subject of an early knitting duel in my own family. In about 1928, my two knitting great grandmothers paid a visit to the family farm to lend a hand for a few weeks. They took to their needles, probably to avoid quarreling, and each produced a complete snow outfit for one of their granddaughters. Each tried to outdo the other. One worked as many differently coloured stripes of Briggs & Little yarn as possible into her creation. The other found some extra special buttons that she sacrificed for the cause. Their granddaughters were the real winners.

My mother (left) and aunt (right) wearing hand-knit snowsuits.

Bootees and socks grew to many different lengths, and full "leggings" could be knit to protect the newly ambulatory. "Girl's spats" were particularly elegant little leggings, painstakingly knit with a foot shaping that covered the instep but stopped before heels and toes. Four carefully placed ties made it possible to anchor the spats to an active leg, and an attractive little shoe could be worn over them for all to see. Designer dressing for children, it seems, is not so new.

Sex-role stereotyping in children's clothes is also not new, but in times past it did not begin as early as today. Toddlers had well-differentiated garments, but an infant was an infant, and most early patterns called only for white yarn and avoided the sex and colour issue entirely. In a time when people had many children to clothe, largely by their own handwork, it was not wise to have too many predispositions on these questions. Nor were there special stitches or fibres for each sex. Boys wore lace and angora trim as frequently as girls and were thought to look the better for it. This makes it difficult when looking at older pattern books to indulge in the popular pastime of telling the sex of baby models.

And what models they were! The books are full of smiling babies, sulky babies, scowling babies, imperious babies, and mischievious babies. Even the occasional sleeping baby graces the pleasant pages of old knitting books. No nuance of mood was missed by the exceptional photographers of yesterday. Babies have always been charmers, but it is quite remarkable to note just how early they had also become fashion plates in Canada. How likely it is, too, that some of these beguiling models sit in the boardrooms of Canada today.

The baby clothes of yesterday were the glorious knitting of their time: consummate expressions of the knitter's art, frothy confections of lace, satin trim, and decorative embroidery. No wool was too fine, no stitch too intricate, and no tailoring too troublesome when it came to clothing the hope for Canada's future. Baby knits were indeed, as one book so perfectly phrased it, "treasures for a woman's greatest treasure."

Knitting for the Baby Boom

The impact of the post World War II baby boom on Canadian society has been profound. Indeed, we continue to feel repeated aftershocks as the great population bubble moves on through time, altering every aspect of society that preceded it. After World War II, the market for hand-knitting patterns and yarns was largely fuelled by the baby boom, to the extent that fashion patterns for

This handsome young chap, dressed in knits, was a contestant in a Canadian National Exhibition baby contest. As his expression indicates, he was not a winner.

adults very nearly disappear from the scene for a number of years. Old pattern books like *Beehive for Bairns* were reprinted and many new ones published.

With the baby boom in full swing by 1947, one journalist tackled the topic for *Macleans Magazine* and offered some impressive statistics. "Nearly 300,000 new Canadians are on the way, scheduled to arrive some time this year," he wrote. In other words, a new baby would be born in Canada every two minutes. The lying-in period in hospitals was reduced from ten days to seven because of the shortage of hospital beds. Statistically, the most popular names for boys were William, John, James, George, and Charles; for girls they were Mary, Elizabeth, Margaret and Helen.[48]

Every new citizen would need approximately thirteen diapers per day. "Running a baby is a full time job," stated *Macleans*. "It takes nearly 6 hours a day, with the equivalent of one of these days each week devoted to washing some of the 3,600 diapers needed during baby's first hectic year." Soaker knitters had plenty to keep them occupied.

When we consider that few parents endeavoured to limit themselves to one postwar baby, the workload seems staggering. Parents even turned competitive, ostensibly on behalf of their offspring, and contests for the most beautiful baby were held. They gave their all to it, and the annual baby contest held at the Canadian National Exhibition in Toronto claimed to be the world's largest.

The Royal Layette Comes to Canada

To Canadians, however, the most interesting baby born during these highly fertile times was not a Canadian. It was HRH Prince Charles, born November 14, 1948. On a visit to England, one privileged but now anonymous knitter from Canada managed to catch a glimpse of the royal layette knit for the new prince. She does not tell us how she managed this, but Canadian knitters are known for their resourcefulness. When she returned home, she transcribed the pattern from memory, and it was widely published in a Newlands baby book so that every Canadian woman might "knit this Royal set for the king in your family." What would Freud have said?

Canadians have always felt themselves to be on very intimate terms with the royal family and have shared their joys and sorrows as though they were all members of the same extended family. Ray Guy, the Newfoundland humourist, tells a story that illustrates this world view perfectly.

When just five years old, he was given the tremendous grown up opportunity of cultivating his own potato patch. This he did, watering, weeding, and fertilizing it with great care and according to the counsel of an oldtimer in the community. The harvest was glorious, and the young farmer glowed with pride. It was wartime, however, and all the talk in the community was about Britain's need for food. Little Ray was asked to contribute some of his treasured crop to the church Harvest Home service to share it with "those less fortunate." When he showed some reluctance to give up his darling spuds, the oldtimer consoled him with the patriotic words, "Don't worry, they'll be sent off straight over there to Mar'ret Rose and she'll have 'em with a relish for her suppertime."[49]

So a desire to know everything about the new baby and to copy the royal layette came naturally to Canadians. It was a no nonsense layette, much like the lives of the royal children in general. It included a coat with a neat garter stitch collar, a bonnet, bootees, and thumbless mittens with modest little tassels on the wrists. A royal carriage cover was also knit in the same pattern, but of heavier yarn. It was probably rather draughty on the steps of Buckingham Palace when the young prince was put out for his nap. Perhaps too, the pattern writer thought it indelicate to include a pair of royal soakers in the layette.

Because of the resourcefulness of one knitter, many Canadian baby boys were wheeled about this vast young country wearing very distinguished livery indeed.

Canadian Kids' Knits

Baby clothes and baby patterns have stood the test of time, and older patterns are constantly recycled and re-knit today with great pleasure. The greatest change in knitting design, however, has come in the area of children's clothes. Gone are the simple knee socks, the Fair Isle vests, and short pants of yesterday. Dino the Dinosaur has replaced Little Tommy Tucker.

We know that in most periods of history children were viewed as tiny adults and dressed accordingly, but we would surely be surprised to realize how well this philosphy has survived in our own times. The pattern books show it clearly. Until very recent times, children's patterns were echoes of the tailored, sombre coloured cardigans, vests, and pullovers of adult clothes. Mother and daughter look-alike dressing was no accident. Little girls were encouraged to emulate their mother's appearance as well as her actions from the very start. Little boys' Sunday best included starched shirts, tailored jackets, and miniature ties. It is as though childhood were mere preparation for adulthood rather than a time with a quality, an imagination, and tastes of its own. The "training for reigning" implication of children's knitted fashions in past times was unmistakable — the fun was already over; adulthood next stop.

There may perhaps be another explanation for the severity of children's clothing in past years. There was no television to supply a world of life, colour, and imagery designed especially for the minds of children. They were not considered to be a market segment with powers of choice or influence over their practical parents. We know better today. The arrival of children's programming and

Earlier children's knits were designed to make them look and behave like small adults.

the opportunity of directly influencing their tastes, preferences, and therefore their parents' purchasing decisions, changed all that.

Whatever the reason, today's rich world of kids' knits is exciting, stimulating, and appealing to even the most traditional of knitting grandmothers. Bright colours, exotic images, and adventurous shapes characterize the new tempo of

Children's sweaters today are full of colour, life, and distinctive imagery.

children's knitting. An unprecedented abundance of easy care yarns invites ambitious knitting, not washday headaches. Sweaters today speak to children's minds about the colour and design of the world — they do not simply keep them warm.

At the far end of the spectrum of childhood lies the other neglected age group for knitters of times past — the teenager. Until our own times, no one dreamed that teenagers might have a lively and independent fashion sense, let alone the economic wherewithal to gratify it. Few patterns were designed for young people and those that were were merely children's patterns made longer or adult's patterns made shorter. There was little to distinguish the one from the other. There was little concession to the notion that this was a distinctly formative and creative period of life. It was assumed that somewhere around the age of eighteen children would slip quietly into the adulthood for which they had been preparing for so long.

The shoe is on the other foot today, and rock and roll is here to stay. The ideas, styles, and energies of young people drive the fashion industry, and many of us must be careful indeed to avoid the "mutton dressed as lamb" syndrome. However, every one of us must agree on one thing — the exuberance of a youth-led fashion industry gives us a brighter, more vivid world to live and knit in.

Solomon in All His Glory: Men's Dress Socks

Socks and Sartorial Giddiness

Men of the Middle Ages and Renaissance were the fashion plates and strutting popinjays of their times. Coloured hose, luxuriously draped sleeves, fabrics richly embroidered in bright jewel tones, the softest of leathers, and the most exotic of feathers and trims adorned the male of the species. If this seems strange to us in the workaday world of the 1990s, we must remember that masculine bombast of many types is not without precedent in the natural world. In fact, we are told that it is not an end in itself but that it serves the rather useful purpose of attracting a mate. Why then should men's clothing not reflect this high purpose?

One remnant of the male love of ostentatious finery most certainly remains. It is the gentle-

men's hand-knit sock — not the humble work sock, but rather those splendid birds of paradise, the pair of dress socks. As finely worked as the robe of an oriental potentate, a mere glance through the pattern books shows us that Solomon in all his glory was not arrayed as well as the foot of the average Canadian man.

After baby patterns, more patterns for dress socks have been published over the years than for any other garment. And like baby patterns, the love and care lavished on their making defies the limits of today's utilitarian imagination. For it must be said that hand-knit socks were the first casualty of the throwaway clothing economy and that these splendid anachronisms are essentially preposterous today.

Why preposterous? A beautifully patterned pair of socks takes a great many hours to make. They require special care in washing and drying. And, like an expensive car, they are subjected to very hard use and need highly skilled repairs. Finally, their glorious light is usually hidden under a bushel, for many men now spend their days sitting cramped behind office desks, not with their legs stretched out luxuriously before the fire with their socks exposed for all the world to see.

With that predictable defiance of logic that drives popular taste, this of course means that the rage for exotic hand-knit socks is gaining in momentum. None other than Peter Gzowski, Canada's foremost radio personality, numbered hand-knit socks among his ten favourite things in the book *Hooray for Canada*.

But unlike today's expensive cars, fancy dress socks can scarcely be had for love or money. As a status symbol and as a proof of love, they are unequalled, for not many girls today spend their spare hours knitting argyles for their boyfriends as their mothers did. And those wives and mothers who may still have the unenviable job of laundering most socks will certainly not knit them. They could not bear to see the inevitable physical abuse heaped upon their careful work.

Many of today's women would be deaf to the eloquent appeal found in early versions of the much published *Socks By Beehive* series.

You want to knit HIM a pair of socks? If he likes to express his individuality in gay colour effects and patterns you will find socks galore throughout this book to satisfy his sartorial giddiness.

But it is as an art form rather than as a practical garment that the hand-knit sock is unsurpassed. The elegant dress socks of yesterday were

A scene not often played out in homes today. Father's splendid footwear illustrates the high art of sock knitting in times past.

personalized by knitted monograms or by the symbols of a man's leisure life — playing cards, bowling balls, and such. Shamrocks, thistles, roses, or the maple leaf might indicate one's country of origin or of choice. Socks were checked, flecked, harlequined, herringboned, or sumptuously striped in a dozen intricate ways. They might also be part of a matching labour-of-love ensemble that included socks, gloves, and scarf.

Innovations in Sock Knitting

The great popularity of sock knitting and sock wearing was bound to attract the energies of the improvers. Patons & Baldwins stepped in to improve wearability. The Beehive Aladdin Heel was a virtually magical way of replacing a worn heel or toe without re-knitting the entire foot. Knitters seized on this concept as a drowning man would seize an outstretched hand. The effectiveness of the Aladdin heel depended on the unravelling of the worn parts of the knitting, according to a pre-designed plan. Stitches were then picked up in pre-ordained places and the heel re-knit. The final step was the grafting of the new to the old stitches, a truly comfortable and seamless method of finishing a sock. The inventors said this of their design:

By making the replacement of heels in socks a simple and practical operation, Patons & Baldwins Limited are glad to offer this contribution toward your personal economy.

Being canny businessmen, they also said:

An application for patent has been filed and although Patons & Baldwins Limited welcome the use of this invention by persons knitting socks by hand with Patons & Baldwins' yarn, other persons should not use or imitate this invention without first obtaining a license in writing from Patons & Baldwins Limited.

Perhaps when all the work was done, the knitters of the Aladdin heel hoped to encourage the wearers of the Aladdin heel to spend more time flying on carpets and less time walking on their socks.

The Beehive Innovation Sock was a development of equal consequence to the knitting world. Its inventors must have sensed that they were onto something because they used strong language indeed when describing this marvel. "If you are one of the many constant Beehive sock knitters," they said, "you will rejoice with us that we have found a new way for you to knit the time-honoured sock."

It was a three-step method. The sock was knit on two needles, thus making beautiful patterns accessible to even the less skilled. A T-shaped piece that covered the instep and the front of the ankle was knit first. Stitches at the toe end were picked up and knit down and around the sole of the foot to the heel, then up the back of the ankle, shaping carefully all the way. Finally, the seams were sewn together invisibly. A patent was applied for once again.

Both inventions underline the fearful geometry of the sock and how well our foremothers knew it. Sock knitting was high art, almost unequalled in today's knitting. And all to cover that most utilitarian of body parts, a man's foot.

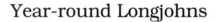

Year-round Longjohns

If handsome dress socks were the zenith of knitting for men, longjohns must be the nadir of their sartorial cosmos. Even in our present century, Canadian men wore hand-knit underwear. Hand-knit, knee-length underwear was one of the first garments to be produced by the Cowichan Indian knitters of British Columbia. They were knit in the round with ribbed portions at the cuffs and waistband and a finely tapered inseam on the legs. The crotch was comfortably shaped and the fly

opening and waistband were skillfully bound with fabric and buttoned. There was no sign of a convenient trap door.

On the opposite coast, some men wore longjohns in summer as well as in winter. Newfoundland folklorist Hilda Chaulk Murray wrote that her grandfather, a very large man, wore his longjohns all year round, being a firm believer in the principle that "what will keep out the cold will keep out the heat." He may not have been comfortable all the time, but he was certainly right and in good company. Sheiks on the best dressed lists of the Arabian Peninsula wear finely woven wool robes, turbans, and burnooses to insulate themselves from the scorching desert sun by day and the cold air by night. Not only does wool slow down the transmission of heat from the body outwards but the reverse is also true.

Were longjohns itchy? Our pampered and ultrasensitive skins of today would doubtless find them so, but we must remember that the fabric grew softer with each laundering and with near constant wear. A man's longjohns began to feel like a second skin after a time and a newly knit pair was more to be endured than heartily welcomed. And so some discriminating wearers refused to be parted from them, summer or winter.

Longjohns were not only worn by men. The *Universal Knitting Book*, a popular turn-of-the-century pattern book often used in Canada, had an entire chapter on underwear for all the family, including patterns for "lady's combinations," "lady's drawers," and children's long underwear. Longjohns are, of course, standard issue for women in Canada's frigid zones. Georgia, the Arctic journalist, described her hurried preparations for going on an impromptu hunting expedition not so long ago.

I burst into my house and hastily turned it upside down, strewing clothes, food, and gear all over. I donned several layers of clothing, starting with the long johns I had just finished knitting, and stuffed extra kamiks, duffel stockings, mitts and scarf, and a pound of raisins, a package of dried fruit, the remains of a box of crackers, camera film, and metal cup into a small mail bag.[50]

Did Georgia mean full-length underwear, surely a great labour to knit by hand, or did she perhaps mean those popular garments once known as "snuggees," or just plain "bloomers"? Knitting patterns for this class of underwear abound, and not in yesterday's instruction books alone. Nevertheless, in times past, when women knit their own

Lynn Maclachlan's delightful sweater is a visual witticism in yarn.

An imaginative rendering of
the Woolmark symbol.

underthings, they usually had something a bit more delicate in mind.

⬭〜⬭〜⬭

The Secret Life of Knitting: Intimate Apparel for Ladies

Susanna Moodie was of the opinion that Canadian women were over fond of dressing ostentatiously and that they often jeopardized their husbands' incomes because of this weakness of character, but she grudgingly awarded us rather high marks for our taste in selecting colours. She made it clear too that our vanities did not extend to our underwear. This is certainly not true today, but perhaps it was more credible in the years before we sustained the collective fear of car accidents in which our lingerie would be found wanting.

Among the [Canadian] women, a love of dress exceeds all other passions. In public they dress in silks and satins, and wear the most expensive ornaments, and they display considerable taste in the arrangement and choice of colours. The wife of a man in moderate circumstances, whose income does not exceed two or three hundred pounds a-year, does not hesitate in expending ten or fifteen pounds upon one article of outside finery, while often her inner garments are not worth as many sous; thus sacrificing to outward show all the real comforts of life.[51]

What a shocking accusation of frivolity and of insubstantial moral development among our foremothers! Perhaps Susanna did not keep sufficient company with the knitting classes, for early instruction books are full of complicated patterns for elegant intimate apparel.

That women's undergarments are engineering marvels was no less true in times past. *The Workwoman's Guide*, for example, recommends the knitting of a "little habit shirt." These are "set close to the chest and give a great deal of warmth." Another item, called simply "a bosom friend," is not explained nor are any indelicate illustrations given, but some interesting if cryptic instructions are provided for the knitter: "Sew pieces of white ribbon to the corners, to hang it by round the neck," and "Some persons do not hollow out bosom friends, but knit them square or oblong."

Hosiery

Every woman needed stockings to wear and garters to secure them, but the author of *The Workwoman's Guide* shared Susanna's retrogressive feelings about knitting and social standing.

Knit stockings are considered so much better than woven ones for wear, that it is advisable for all servants, cottagers and labourers invariably to adopt them, as the former will last out three or more of the woven, which are more suitable for the higher classes. The children of the poor should always be taught to knit, and each member of a family ought to have a stocking in hand to take up at idle moments...

Such prejudices vanished when women of different backgrounds began to share common life experiences in the new country, and the time came when stockings could be both knit and worn by one and all without fear of social reprisals. Moreover, beautiful stockings became an art form. Fine cotton knitting yarns had become common in Europe in the latter part of the eighteenth century, and they were plentiful and affordable in Canada by the nineteenth century. Beautifully patterned wedding gloves and long lacy stockings were knit from silk or cotton, sometimes using fine pieces of piano wire for needles. Girls spent years filling their hope chests, or at least their bottom drawers, with such intimate delicacies.

Perhaps the *pièce de résistance* in fine ladies' hosiery was a pair of gaiters. A pattern for these appeared in *Home Work: A Choice Collection of Useful Designs for the Crochet and Knitting Needle*, published in Toronto in 1891. A gaiter was a complex stocking with no sole but with a perfectly shaped instep, much like spats. It extended to just below the knee. The top was delicately ribbed, as was a section around the ankle. The middle of the stocking and the instep were both highly patterned in different lace stitches. Standards of propriety of the time dictated that ankles be thoroughly covered at all times, but the ornamentation on a pair of gaiters suggests that the women of yesterday took every possible opportunity to flash their ankles.

Accessories

The nineteenth century was the heyday of decorative lace knitting, so the more visible parts of a lady's body were given attractive and winsome knitted lace coverings as well. We may assume that ladies' "wristers" and "wristlets" were primarily decorative and shared nothing but a name with the coarse woollen ones worn by fishermen. A knitted "muffatee," shortened in later times to "muff," kept the hands of the fairer sex warm and attractive when the cold became more serious.

Ladies must have often fluttered their delicate hands in order to draw attention to their craftsmanship. Indeed, knitting itself was thought to add grace to a lady's movements in the way that a male bird dances to attract a mate. We can but speculate on the role that knitting played in courtship in Canada.

Lace nightcaps and headscarves were needed too. One of the latter was called a "zephyrine" and was described as "a very convenient thing to lie over the head instead of a bonnet, especially in travelling." These later came to be called "fascinators," and a more evocative name for an item of fine ladies' apparel cannot be imagined.

Ladies' Comforters

In the days before women wore sweaters to keep warm, shawls did the job, and the art of shawl knitting was as popular in Canada as it was in Europe. A shawl, of course, does not really need to fit anyone in particular, and for this reason knitters have often made them as a showcase for their improvisational skill.

Shawls of different types were distinguished by their dimensions and by the way they were draped. Some drapings were very novel indeed. The "tippet" was a short circular shawl covering the shoulders only. *The Workwoman's Guide* of 1840 says that "neat tippets might be made with advantage for school girls at times when worsteds are cheap."

There are also many patterns for small shawls called "comforters," whose warming benefits were local rather than general. One of these patterns

In the era before sweater dressing became popular for women, ladies wore finely knitted lace shawls to keep warm and to showcase their skills.

begins, "For one comforter, buy a quarter of a pound of lamb's wool." The sketch shows a simple rectangle that could be wound closely around the neck as a scarf or worn about the shoulders as a stole. Another pattern shows a circular tube of knitting that was drawn over the head and an attached chest piece that hung down the front. This comforter was just the thing for wearing inside a handsome coat. It must have been considered something rather special for the instructions read, "This is knit with soft wool and upon ivory pins."

A fine lace shawl was a garment of distinction, but for everyday wear or for the woman with a lot of work to do, something more practical was needed. The "ladies' nightingale" was a shawl that was tapered along the arms to cuffed wrists. The resulting garment, a shawl with sleeves, was an obvious improvement. Housework could be done, pots could be stirred, and fires could be stoked without the troublesome ends of a shawl dangling in the way.

In the Maritime provinces this garment went by the cosy name of a "hug-me-tight." In her diary, Lucy Maud Montgomery mused about whether her children and grandchildren would remember her as a "thin, wrinkled, little, gray-haired body, always sitting in a warm corner, with a hug-me-tight on, reading a book...." One thing is certain — no Canadian ever pictured the author of the immensely popular *Anne of Green Gables* in this self-abnegating pose. Interestingly enough, Lucy Maud went on to declare, "If ever I *am* a grandmother I am going to do nothing but read books and do filet crochet!" She craved leisure time for needlework.

Unlike its earlier hardworking sisters, the frilly bedjacket brought the tradition of wearing intimate knitted lace into our own times. Photographs of these confections, so delicately knit and with such limited usefulness, give an impression of gracious living and an abundance of leisure time that few people ever experienced in Canada at any time.

The need for something to wear when resting up during a difficult pregnancy or while nursing a baby in the middle of a cold night was probably the real reason for the popularity of bedjackets. Nevertheless, wearing a work of knitted art must have made many women feel a bit pampered, even if for only a few days here and there.

Fascinators, nightingales, and zephyrines...the language of yesterday's intimate apparel is as sibilant as silk, alluring, yet cloaked in secrecy, suggesting a feminine mystique of days gone by. The hard lives of many women were doubtless softened by knitting something precious and dainty.

Cutting A Fine Figure: The Canadian Woman of Fashion

Not all Canadian knits were created equal. Life in the drawing rooms, the salons, the parlours, and the resorts of the nation demanded chic, sophisticated, and unique clothes that fulfilled the fashion expectations of Canadian women. Knitters took up the challenge. Besides, Canadian women did not want to spend all their time knitting for their husbands, their children, and their home. There was a larger world to conquer.

The Cosmopolitan Knitter

In the fashion conscious twenties, Canadian hand knits for women opened a window on the world of fashion. The introduction to a Monarch knitting book of 1924 confidently declared:

In this special book we illustrate the very latest styles created by Jeane Duncan for Spring and Summer, from ideas gathered in American and European warm climate Winter Resorts, and they are the coming vogue.

Cosmopolitan they certainly were. The "Mandarin Coat," the "Mah Jong Sweater," the "tuxedo," and the numerous patterns for little "jaquettes" of one type or another suggested fashion aspirations and cultural ties that were not just plain Canadian.

Gone too were instructions calling for materials like "a little light lambswool" that could be found on the family farm. Knitters of the roaring twenties used romantic yarns named "Starlight," "Crepe Silk," and "Silvertwist" in complex shades like "helio," "cherry," and "lavender."

A mere decade later, the bubble burst and the experience of worldwide economic vulnerability replaced some fashion fantasies with more common sense garments. Women began to knit their own two- and three-piece suits and dresses, tailoring them smartly with knitted gores, darts, and trims. These garments were marvels of fit, shaping, and finishing, seldom equalled in the knitting world. Pattern names also became a little less exotic and nearer perhaps to one's personal experience of travel. Patterns in the 1938 *Lux Knitting Book*, for example, were named Laurentian, Jasper, Atlantic, and Pacific.

Many Canadians got their first exposure to luxury fibres by knitting angora sweaters.

The Sweater Look

Shortages of yarn in the consumer market caused fashion knitting in the 1940s to sink a considerable distance into the wartime abyss, but it rebounded with vigour soon after. The "sweater look" became the universal norm for female dressing and yarn sales soared. Form-fitting cardigans and neatly sculptured pullovers with impossibly tiny waists were designed to cling to curves that were meant to look generous. Not only were these sweaters an apex of knitted perfection but the foundation garments that sustained them presumably had miraculous properties, for there were never any wrinkles or inappropriate bulges on a sweater girl.

A soft look came to women's wear with the rage for angora sweaters in the 1950s. Sweaters today might incorporate a touch of angora in strategic places, but yesterday's garments were made entirely of pure angora. It was tossed about with abandon in full-length cabled cardigans and stranded thickly into elaborate but casual Fair Isle designs. It was used to indulge children and to spoil them forever with an unforgettable taste of luxury. Worse still, it sometimes decorated ignominious parts of the body like the legs and feet. Such profligacy can scarcely be imagined today, but angora yarn was once as affordable as it was popular.

Accessories

Superb accessories were a social passport to the aspiring woman of fashion who never left home without them. *Hand In Glove With Beehive* struck the right tone on the significance of gloves:

> *Your hand knit gloves can be just as aristocratic as your ensemble...the caressing warmth of a hand shake speaks comfort to a friend. Let the caressing warmth of Beehive speak comfort to your hands.*

Women could make all their own accessories, but surely only the most careful and most disciplined of knitters did. The instructions were extraordinarily demanding. One such pattern, "Lady's Gloves with a Frilled Cuff," was knit on four needles, at a tension of thirty stitches to four inches, and had different instructions for each finger. "Lady's Fureen Striped Gloves" were knit at thirty-six stitches to four inches, had the palm side worked in one solid colour, and the front of the gloves striped lengthwise from fingertip to cuff in five different shades. The challenge of length-

wise stripes alone would madden many of today's knitters.

Chapeaux

The culmination of the fashion knitter's art was the making of hats — not the everyday Canadian toque or tam o'shanter, but the ambitious little "Winged Pill Box," the "Turban," and the "Lace Cloche." The makers of these astonishing creations virtually needed certification in two trades — millinery as well as knitting. Special materials and advanced skills were needed. Wire was used to stiffen brims and to give added firmness to the finished shapes. Beading, braiding, tufting, and ruching were all used to add ornamental details. Tassels and pompoms were wrapped with gold thread before being invisibly attached to their chapeau. Knitting a hat was certainly not the work of an evening or two, it was more like the project of a lifetime.

And what can be said of the results? A hat is a garment that makes its own statement, and some of these speak rather alarmingly of the fashions, sensibilities, and lifestyles of days gone by. Others speak of original and imaginative ways to frame the human face and to draw attention to its universal appeal. All advertise the skill and ambition of their makers.

Wearing well-made garments knit from quality yarns, carefully accessorised, and fastidiously groomed, the Canadian woman of fashion felt ready to go anywhere.

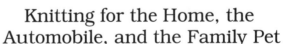

Knitting for the Home, the Automobile, and the Family Pet

In the early days, women who could spare the time knit for their homes as much as for their families. It was socially acceptable to knit while entertaining company in the parlour during an evening, but propriety dictated that this be "fancy work," usually for the home, never an item of intimate apparel. A knitted lace "doyley" or "fancy" was just the thing, and the great number of these found in museums today is a testimony to their one-time popularity — and to the quietness of the countless evenings without television that produced them. Doilies are still beautiful today and old patterns are as luxurious as new. These webs of lace beautified many homes that were probably rather rough and hard to keep clean.

Bedcoverings, known sometimes as coverlets, counterpanes, and even "quilts" were knit from fine, if inexpensive, white cotton. (The term "afghan" dates from our time and its origins are obscure.)

Bedcoverings were usually knit one square at a time on very fine needles so they made suitable drawing room work. On Tuesday, January 27, 1914, Lucy Maud Montgomery began a knitting project that meant so much to her that she recorded it in her diary — knitters often do keep track of the momentous beginnings and climactic endings of their best work.

Today I began to knit a quilt. That sounds like an arrant folly in a woman who is as busy as I am....

Quilt knitting, in this particular pattern especially always makes me think of Malpeque [P.E.I.]...every girl and woman in Malpeque had knitted, was knitting, or intended to knit a quilt — some of them several quilts. They possessed many patterns and considerable rivalry went on. Lace knitting was very popular also. I caught the fever and began a quilt. I think I was three years knitting it. It was very pretty but was worn out long ago. Ten years ago I knitted a second which I still have. Shall I ever finish a third? [52]

The time required to knit a work of sculptured beauty like the Cape Spear coverlet must also be measured in years. Cape Spear, located on the very edge of Newfoundland, is the easternmost

The Cape Spear coverlet was made of 1,536 shell-shaped pieces, which were knit individually and then sewn together. It required an estimated eight hundred hours to complete. It is on display today in the Cape Spear lighthouse.

point of North America. It is the site of an isolated lighthouse that has been in operation since 1834. In recent years, the building has been restored and the Cape Spear coverlet is displayed in the master bedroom of the lighthouse. It consists of 1,536 shell-shaped pieces that were knit individually and then sewn together. The quality of the cotton thread used in the coverlet was very high, and though it is more than a century old, it has no areas of weakness or breakage. It is estimated that it took eight hundred hours of hand knitting to make the Cape Spear coverlet. How thrilling it is to imagine the keeper's wife working by candle or lamplight, night after night, to beautify her rugged and isolated home. The pattern is available today — for those who have the time.

Automobile Knits

It is difficult for most of us today to conceive of life in a time without the automobile. In fact, today's reader of nineteenth century knitting patterns who comes upon a pattern for "driving mitts" must read the words "knit the remainder in imitation double knitting, which is not so clumsy for the palm of the hand when grasping reins..." in order to remember that there are older meanings of the verb "to drive."

Patterns for car rugs were published as early as the 1920s, when motoring was thought to be a glamorous alternative to traditional forms of transportation. Automobiles themselves were luxurious and people of means frequently had them built to their own specifications. Motoring, though perhaps thrilling, was also hazardous and cold work. People dressed in special clothes that were warm and windproof and kept out the dust. Today, driving has become a mere necessity, not an activity worthy of a knitter's attention. It may, in fact, rob the knitter of valuable time better spent with the needles.

Fido Knits

Where did the idea of knitting for dogs first appear? It would not seem to be a Canadian invention. Until recent times, most descendants of the wolf residing in Canada were hardy farm dogs who lived an outdoor life and who earned their keep as working dogs. The change came with the growing popularity of small breeds of companionable dogs and with a change to urban apartment living. Fido knits date, however, from the 1920s when they were invariably sized to fit a "Scotty dog," doubtless one of Canada's first pampered pets.

Fido knits are big business today. The Cumberland County Knitters of Wallace, Nova Scotia, produce Canada's most sought after dog sweater, a pure wool extravaganza of colour. First displayed at the Toronto Boat Show, demand has grown to unprecedented heights. In one year alone, the company supplied three hundred dog sweaters to Holt Renfrew's prestigious Toronto department store and 1,200 additional sweaters to equally prestigious canine boutiques. Cumberland County says that a knitter can make two small dog sweaters in one day, but that it takes one full day to make a medium or large Fido knit.

The tables have been turned. Where man's best friends once worked for us, we now work to keep them elegantly attired and living in the lap of luxury.

Knitted Novelties: The World of the Tea Cosy

Are some things better left unknit? Even the most enthusiastic knitter of today must surely believe so. In modern times, a careful weighing of the expenditure of time against the usefulness of the object to be knit has eliminated many unworthy items from the pantheon of knitted novelties.

Our foremothers did not agree. Nothing was too much trouble for them, and anything that prevented the outflow of money from the home was worth making. Unlike women of today, their time was not a commodity that had a potential cash value.

One of the patterns in *The Workwoman's Guide* of 1840 illustrates this notion. It is for knitted pen wipes, undoubtedly one of the least productive uses of the time of any knitter of any generation. Further consideration of the merits of the knitted pen wipe tempts the modern knitter to make free with Shakespeare and to conclude that "if it were knit, then 'twere well it were knit quickly."

Not all nineteenth century novelties were so pedestrian. One issue of *Godey's Magazine and Lady's Book* contained published patterns for "knitted berries and fruit," including "holly and its berries" and "mistletoe and its berries." The printed instructions for one single holly berry required twelve whole lines of minute type. No detail was thought too fine or too picayune to be spared. The pattern for the mistletoe berry reads:

Make the berries in white China silk, exactly

*like those of the holly; the little spot at the top
brown instead of black; no stem.*

No knitter would wish to be thought botanically
incorrect.

Some novelties of the nineteenth century were
much more functional. We find patterns for "ladies' knee caps," body belts for every member of
the family, and the "knit armlet," which could be
worn by "little children, in severe weather, over
their little naked arms to prevent them from chap-
ping."

Elegant accessories for the man or woman of
fashion might also be knit. An abundance of patterns were published for the lady's silken "reticule
bag," gentlemen's braces, which could be knit
from wool, cotton, or silk, and men's knitted neck-
ties. These intricately crafted items probably made
suitable parlour knitting projects on those occasions when the lady of the house did not wish to
be seen working on her pen wipe.

That universal proof of the ability to knit, the
pot holder, first appears in printed patterns in the
mid-nineteenth century. Simple necessity suggests much earlier beginnings, but the idea of
using decorative stitches and colours came along
in these later times. The first patterns were called
"kettle holders" and have the familiar tab that
makes a pot holder ready to hang on its hook by
the stove.

The "flower stand cover" was a knitted tube
made to cover a rough container in which flowers
were planted. This multi-coloured and fringed
extravaganza of the knitter's art may in fact have
been an antecedent of the toilet roll cover of our
times. This sobering thought should keep us from
becoming too superior in our attitude toward the
novelties of yesterday. We must remember too
that today's kitsch may well be considered
tomorrow's folk art.

In fact, the knitted novelties of our own time are
no more believable than those of the nineteenth
century. The Monarch Knitting Company's 1944
book of *Knitted Gift Suggestions* gives instructions
for a window blind pull, ornamental hot water
bottle covers of every description, a baby bottle

Tea cosies were often designed to appeal to a knitter's flights
of fancy.

cover, and a powder can cover. Indeed, the urge to cover seems to be a powerful motive for knitters of novelties and bric-a-brac of all generations. Moreover, all pattern books provide instructions for that most redundant of all novelties, the knitted knitting bag.

Tea Cosies

The American travel writer Paul Theroux, after puzzling over the character of the English, concluded that they were a most unusual nation because they kept their homes so cold but put lavishly made cosies on their tea pots. The tea cosy is undoubtedly one of Britain's legacies to its far flung empire.

According to the *Oxford English Dictionary*, the derivation of the word "cosy" is unknown, but it is thought to relate to a Gaelic word meaning "sheltered, snug, or warm." Its earliest recorded use in a knitting context was in 1863, when one man wrote: "It is not unusual to preserve the heat of teapots by a woollen covering but the 'cosy' must fit loosely." An 1886 advertisement in an English newspaper promoted "tea-coseys" in the company of those other distinguished knitted novelties, the cushion and the antimacassar.

In Canada, patterns for the knitted tea cosy and its tinier companion, the egg cosy, were in wide circulation by 1900. The *Universal Knitting Book*, one of the earliest instruction books sold in Canada by Patons & Baldwins, includes patterns for two tea cosies (one inexplicably designed for "bachelors"), one coffee-pot cosy, and one hot-water jug cosy. The Canadian tea drinking ceremony could scarcely be compared in intricacy to the Japanese; nevertheless, no ingredient in this important rite of refreshment was abandoned to the cold.

Not much has changed about the tea cosy in our own times. Ribbed or stripped, crusted with pompoms, flowers, or leaves, disguised as an artichoke or a night cap, they are a throwback to earlier decorative sensiblities. But they do still keep the tea warm.

Dolls' Clothes

For another group of novelty knitters, artistry is particularly important. They are the dolls' clothes knitters; a group whose sincere interest in miniaturization is all that sets them apart from the skilled fashion knitters of adult clothing today. Dolls' clothes are every bit as intricate and skill testing. They must also fit properly. The only real difference is that their wearers do not complain if something is amiss.

People have made dolls' clothes for as long as there have been dolls. Historians and anthropologists tell us that this is a very long time indeed. Dolls' clothes knitters, and there are a great many of them today, tend to be specialists who enjoy executing fine detail in miniature. Some are known to knit miniature Shetland lace shawls on needles as fine as wire.

They find a further challenge in clothing different types of dolls, for dolls and their wardrobes have lived through fashion cycles comparable to those of their mistresses. They may begin knitting for the nineteenth century china dolls that were the models for all successive baby dolls. The knitting patterns of our day were written for dolls that have already grown into small children and must wear tiny perfect pleated skirts, Fair Isle sweaters, and berets.

Perhaps the consummate expression of the miniaturist's art is creating a wardrobe for a teenage doll. These dolls have been popular for thirty years, as Barbie's recent birthday reminds us. Mary Maxim's masterful *Teen Age Doll Book*, which dates from the beginning of that period, included patterns for a Chanel-style suit, pillbox hat, Bermuda shorts, and many purses. Ensembles were trimmed with embroidery, sequins, and pompoms. No detail was too small. The pattern for the entire "girl's off-shoulder dress, hat and purse" called for one quarter ounce of four-ply fingering yarn.

Why do the makers of knitted novelties do it? Why do they use their time, energy, and skill in lavishly ornamenting such expendable items when a wider knitting world calls? After all, many Canadians through the ages have learned to live without a tea cosy.

In early days, the economic motive took precedence over the artistic. People did not have a lot of cash so most things were made at home. Nor did local merchants carry the variety of novelty goods that they do today.

Over the years, the habit of thriftiness has probably been a motivator equal to scarcity of money, although the two do not necessarily go hand in hand. Naturally thrifty knitters feel rewarded when they use scraps of yarn. Today, when vast quantities of excellent, affordable yarn are readily available — and many Canadians are kept gainfully employed producing it — some knitters still do not want to rid themselves of parsimonious inclinations.

One thing is certain. Novelty knitters have never thought that they were wasting their time or skill. Those who give themselves psychological permission to make something small, colourful, and ornamental have found the experience a sustaining diversion, leading from the well-trodden paths of duty knitting into the world of imagination.

Knitting for the Sporting Life

For some people, Canada's many regions, its cool climate, and four splendidly distinct seasons are cause for celebration, not a reason to move to the sun belt. These are the hardy *types sportifs*, the adventurers, the athletes, the outward bound.

Knitting has always gone hand in hand with the sporting life. One early Monarch pattern book summarized the delights of the relationship this way:

> *Golf links and tennis courts, mountain paths and country lanes, ski slopes and ice cushions are calling all active Canadians. For sunny spring days, cool summer evenings, crisp autumn air and invigorating winter's cold, comfortable, cosy-to-wear, smart-looking hand knit sportswear is necessary to the full enjoyment of your favorite sport.*

Knitting has served both summer and winter, team and individual athletic endeavours, but in some particular sporting circles its contribution has been outstanding.

Hockey

Perhaps no garment has been knit in Canada more than the hockey sweater. *The Canadian Encyclopedia* hardly exaggerated the furious rage for our national game when it called it merely "a major winter preoccupation of Canada's male youth for almost 100 years." Hockey was and is a reason for being, a physical and psychological *sine qua non* for most young Canadian men. In his story, *The Hockey Sweater*, author Roch Carrier sums up the relationship in a few simple evocative words:

> *The winters of my childhood were long, long seasons. We lived in three places — the school, the church and the skating rink — but our real life was on the skating rink. Real battles were won on the skating rink. Real strength appeared on the skating rink. The real leaders showed themselves on the skating rink.*[53]

With such fundamental developmental matters at stake, having the correct hockey sweater was of supreme importance in this game that was also a metaphor for life. A young player could not perform unless he was wearing the right team colours, and for young Roch that meant the colours of the Montreal Canadiens. Wearing the wrong colours, the mind and body just could not work together, as he discovered when his mother mistakenly bought him a sweater in the colours of the hated rival team, the Toronto Maple Leafs.

She naturally thought it was a detail of little importance, and like all good mothers with a supreme belief in their children's intrinsic worth she insisted that, "It isn't what's on your back that counts, it's what you've got inside you head."

Roch wore the sweater and the unthinkable happened. He was benched, he was penalized, and he was finally thrown out of the game by the parish priest, who reprimanded him for bad manners on the ice and insisted that he make a full confession to boot. It was a case of simple discrimination. In ignominy and despair, little Roch made his confession and also prayed for deliverance. He asked God to send, as quickly as possible, many moths to eat up his sweater.

Had Madame Carrier knit her son's sweater herself, the problem would not have occurred. The earliest pattern books warned unworldly mothers about the dangers of getting the colours wrong — and thoughtfully named them, for good measure.

> *The boy who is a booster for the Maroons will get a kick out of wearing this three-piece maroon and white hockey set of pullover, toque and stockings. But if your boy's favorite team is the Canadiens knit him this three-piece hockey set...in scarlet, blue and white.*

Today's mothers of tomorrow's National Hockey League stars often feel that they are slaves to the rink, but they are usually hockey's most enthusiastic supporters as well. In past days equal parental dedication was needed, for the amount of work in even one hand-knit hockey set would exhaust any lesser fan.

Curling

Curling was one of the first sports to become popular in colonial Canada. The curling rink, or pond more probably, was also a wonderful showcase for the knitter's skill. Canadians have been involved in international curling competition since Confederation. The game was brought to Canada by the hardy Scots who were no strangers to time-

The hand-knit hockey suit was a labour of love. Thoughtful pattern publishers reminded insouciant knitters of the correct colours for each team.

tested methods of keeping warm in the open air. And since the early sport was always played outdoors in some rather chilly venues, warm clothes were needed.

The first curling sweaters were finely knit, and warm tam o'shanters or toques and matching gloves went with them. The concept of identical team sweaters really became practical when Mary Maxim began publishing its famous sporting sweater patterns in the 1950s. "Curlers! Knit matching Mary Maxim Sweaters in your Club Colours!" its advertisement read.

Several styles were available. One was a ribbed cardigan with deep pockets, knit in lightweight or bulky yarns with lapels, collars, and trim in contrasting team colours. The classic and best known Mary Maxim sweater had the familiar motifs of a stone and crossed brooms on the back, front, and sleeves. The shawl collar and front trim were broadly striped in club colours. A thickly knit

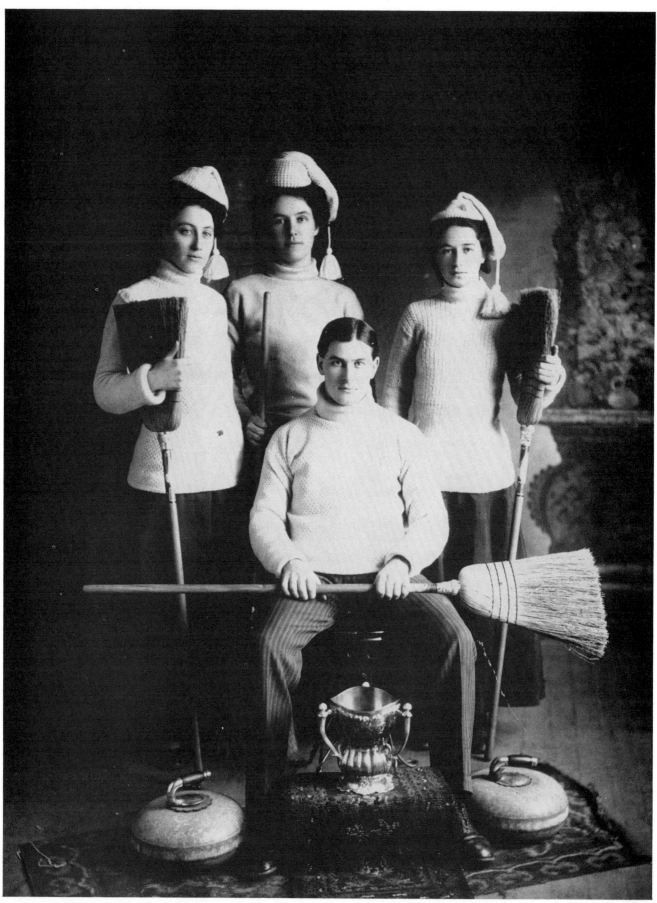

An early curling team dressed in hand knits.

toque completed the outfit. Thousands of these were worn in rinks across the country. Although curling clothes have changed and become more commercialized, especially at higher levels of competition, hand-knit curling sweaters are still often worn and always enjoyed today.

Skating

Among the sporting set, skaters may be Canada's most enthusiastic boosters of hand knitting. Famous skaters often wear beautiful sweaters, and the would-be famous must have them too. This means that the industrious mothers of young skaters are often to be found knitting away the hours in the nation's rinks while their offspring practise their compulsory figures.

Backyard skaters have always wanted warm, lightweight knits because they are ideal clothes for the outdoor ice, but among figure skaters, Barbara Ann Scott may have started the rage. One of Canada's best remembered athletes, she became

Barbara Ann Scott wearing her characteristic knitted angora bandeau. Young skaters wanted to look just like her.

a celebrity when she won the figure skating title at the Olympics in 1948. Her photographs often show her wearing her famous knitted angora bandeau tied firmly under her chin and a short, swinging skating skirt. Thousands of little Canadian girls copied this outfit hoping to copy Barbara's success as well.

Skiing

Experts suggest that skiing was the first European sport to come to Canada. It was brought by the same early Norse peoples who came and went, taking both their knitting and their skis with them, for the tradition of nordic skiing is thought to be four thousand years old. Their descendants who came to Canada in the nineteenth century re-introduced skiing as a practical though rigorous form of winter transportation.

The Canadian Encyclopedia tells us that the first recorded ski outing in Canada occurred in 1879. It was a trip by Mr. A. Birch, a Norwegian gentleman from Montreal, who skiied from Montreal to Quebec City "using a single pole." This feat of skill would seem comparable to knitting a sweater with one needle.

In our own times, Herman Smith (Jackrabbit) Johannsen made traditional cross-country skiing as popular as the alpine variety. Photographs of the energetic Jackrabbit still skiing at ninety years of age inspired old and young alike to take up an obviously salubrious sport and to wear ski sweaters as well.

Where would skiing be without the ski sweater? It is the consummate expression of traditional nordic design and has been copied and worn in all of the world's cold places from Canada to Antarctica. The many nordic-inspired sweaters knit in Canada today are direct descendants of the originals whose crisp, clear motifs celebrate winter in every northern land. With our frosty, star-studded nights and crystal winter days, these sweaters seem to belong here.

Knitting and the Armchair Athlete

Not everyone wants to participate in sports, nor is everyone able to, but people want to look relaxed and sporty, not trussed and formal. Thus garments once knit mainly for the athletic grew into the leisure-wear industry of today. How did this happen?

The early pattern producers were quick to spot this desire, and many ordinary knitted sweaters were made to seem more purposefully athletic than they actually were — possibly because the

"Jackrabbit" Johannsen wearing a hand-knit sweater.

wearers liked to feel and look more athletic than they actually were. By wearing garments similar to those worn by sporting figures, a spectator could actively identify with their sweaty efforts. Being dressed in sympathy meant that spectators could lend athletes an extra measure of vicarious moral support, from a safe distance naturally.

Some early knitting patterns even predicted that phenomenon of our own times, the armchair athlete.

What's your sport? Badminton? Make it in white for that all-over white costume that's so popular. Tennis? Apple green has a cool, refreshing look. Golf? Dutch blue, brick red or tan, whichever suits your summer complexion best. If you prefer to watch rather than play, you'll find a hundred other practical uses for this all purpose pullover.

The armchair athlete is very much a product of the television generation, but we have yet to see a sweater designed especially for watching television.

The 1950s marked the real beginning of the emphasis on hand-knit designer sportswear that continues to flourish. Since style and individuality are often discouraged in working wardrobes, more garments are knit for leisure wear than for formal dressing in Canada today. The emphasis on casual clothing came with postwar economic growth and with the emerging leisure society that the resultant wealth made possible. How curious to think that new wealth, and the cars and televisions that came with it, made the healthy, active, outdoor life so much more difficult to realize.

The Mary Maxim Story

No company had its finger more firmly in place on the racing pulse of the Canadian knitter in the 1950s than Mary Maxim. In other parts of the world, Mary Maxim sweaters became synonyms for Canada. Made with soft, warm wool, even the royals wore them with great pleasure. At home, every Canadian wanted one, from tiny tots to grandparents, and knitters were kept busy making them even for non-knitters and their families. The range of sizes was enormous and those families that enjoyed the feeling of togetherness could wear matching sweaters, but there were enough individual patterns to please the most determined individualist.

Mary Maxim sweaters were the forerunners of today's talking T-shirts. Some patterns were delightful geometrics, but the big successes were the picture knits. If you wanted to advertise your occupation, you might wear a diesel truck on your sweater — in either long nose or snub nose style to prevent mistaken identities of course. No detail was too inconsequential for Mary Maxim's designers. To indicate your hobby, you might have an antique car emblazoned on your back. To advertise your totem animal, you might want to wear a Holstein cow. How did this begin?

It happened in the small town of Sifton, Manitoba, a town far from the corridors of power, but apparently near to the lifespring of the Canadian people. Sifton has a dual distinction — not only did it give birth to Mary Maxim but it was named for Sir Clifford Sifton, the man whose immigration policies were credited with populating the Canadian prairies.

Willard S. McPhedrain, a railway station agent, and his wife Olive lived in Sifton. Willard had an energetic and entrepreneurial mind that was never satisfied with doing just one job at a time, so he and his wife also got involved with a woollen mill and a business known as Sifton Wool Products Ltd. Its major items were blankets, wool batts for quilts, and knitted worksocks. It carried on much of its business by mail, but with rather limited success at first.

One day, a lightening bolt of marketing genius struck Willard — he decided to personalize the appeal of his products. He began to use the name of the family maid, "Miss Mary Maximchuk," to advertise homespun worksocks made by her. Response doubled immediately. After many more successful advertisements were placed, young Mary's personal mail began to get mixed up with the business mail so the name was shortened to "Miss Mary Maxim" and later to the even simpler "Mary Maxim." The company lost some of its prairie flavour in the name change, but none of its momentum.

Some time later, while on a sales trip, a department store clerk showed Willard a pattern graph for a Cowichan sweater. His enquiring mind realized its potential and saw a business opportunity.

This was the origin of Mary Maxim's famous "Graph Style Pattern." The sweaters were lovely, but the patterns alone were such a novelty that many veteran knitters simply had to give them a try. The first pattern produced was No. 400 Reindeer. It is still popular today. Moreover, Mary Maxim sweaters were so well made and wore so well that some of the earliest ones are still in action nearly forty years later.

The demand for yarn and patterns grew so quickly that it might have overwhelmed a less determined business team. A receptive market had been discovered, but finding stable suppliers who could fill orders without delay was a major challenge in this phase of growth. Spinrite Yarns of Listowel, Ontario, undertook the job to produce the famous Northland yarn, and it continues to make it today. In order to be nearer to its suppliers, Mary Maxim moved from Manitoba to Paris, Ontario, in 1954. The rest, as the saying goes, is history.

Willard McPhedrain's son Larry, a telegraph operator and relief station agent at the same railway station as his father before him, joined the business at this time. Willard McPhedrain kept

Swimmer Marilyn Bell wearing her Mary Maxim sweater.

his hands on the wheel until he passed away in 1971 at the age of sixty-eight. His wife and son continue to be active in Mary Maxim today.

Not many Canadians get an opportunity to export their business success, but Mary Maxim did. In 1956, the company began operations in Port Huron, Michigan. The large and prosperous U.S. operation has outgrown its building several times.

Marketing genius put Mary Maxim on the map, but aggressive, expert marketing kept it there and keeps it there today. In the early years, the company began to take part in high profile trade shows in Canada and abroad. These attracted dignitaries by the dozen and soon politicians, movie stars, sports heroes, and princesses were wearing Mary Maxim sweaters. Marilyn Bell, the Toronto swimmer who first conquered the formidable distance of Lake Ontario and became an instant celebrity, often wore one, as did her famous coach Gus Ryder.

In the 1950s, Mary Maxim Ltd. had a sales force that penetrated so deeply into the Canadian hinterland that its sweaters were knit everywhere, from the major cities to the outposts of rural Canada, from cosmopolitan Montreal to the tiniest company towns with no roads. Mary Maxim brought Canadian style to Canadians, no matter where they lived.

Today, the company maintains its market penetration by mailing directly to individual knitters in their homes. Order turnaround time is prompt. Customer service is responsive. And value for money is excellent. Its attractive and ever changing mail-order catalogues reflect the latest and most popular designs on the market today. It keeps those same sensitive fingers on the Canadian knitter's healthy pulse.

CHAPTER 4

Canada's Knitting Yarns And How We Got Them

Until recent decades, wool, silk, and cotton were the primary materials of Canadian knitting. There is no evidence of knitting with mohair or angora before our own times. Silk was used most frequently for making novelty items, fancy stockings, or in bits of delicate lace work. Cotton yarns came into general use in Canada in the latter half of the nineteenth century and were very popular for bedspreads, dressy stockings, and other lace work. However, most garments made in Canada from the earliest colonial times until after World War II were knit from wool.

Wool in Canada

This historic fibre has kept people warm around the world for twelve thousand years, dating from the time, as one writer expressed it, "when man first realized that sheep could be worth more alive than dead."[54]

The arrival of wool in Canada was rather more recent. The French brought sheep with them when they came to the New World. *The Canadian Encyclopedia* tells us that in 1677 there were eighty-five sheep in New France. Sheep may have been farmed in Acadia prior to this, but they were not included in any early census. Twenty years later, the number of sheep had grown to nearly one thousand. By the mid-eighteenth century, there were more than 28,000 grazing in Canadian fields, and sheep farming had become firmly established. Over the years, there have been marked fluctuations in the sheep population, but today there are about 500,000 sheep in Canada. The largest flocks are in Ontario and Alberta.

Canada never became a major wool producing country like Australia or New Zealand. Historically, most families kept only a few head of sheep to produce wool and meat for their own use. In a vivid boyhood memory, Newfoundland humourist Ray Guy summed up the status of sheep on a typical mixed farm.

The setting was a one-room school house on a sunny Friday afternoon in winter. Everyone was longing to be outdoors. The exasperated teacher decided that the time was right to study Shakespeare's celebrated poem about winter. It began:

When icicles hang by the wall,
And Dick, the shepherd, blows his nail...
   [that is, fingernail]

Guy recounts:

That was one tough poem. We struck it in the winter of Grade Eight...

   "What do we mean," the schoolmaster would ask with small hope and for the sake of form, "by 'Dick, the shepherd, blows his nail'?"...

   We all knew what a shepherd was, any fool did. A shepherd was a person who had nothing else to do but tend sheep unless he was a woman in which case he was a shepherdess. Shepherds were persons like Little Bo Peep and David who slew Goliath and damn-his-eyes Dick who blew his nail.

   "Why" was a different matter. Ten or 12 sheep were plenty even for big families. Why would anybody keep so many sheep that it was one person's lifework to tend them? [55]

In past days, most wool was processed at home by individual families. It was part of the seasonal rhythm of life in a Canada that was mostly rural.

Wool Processing on the Family Farm

Sheep were sheared in late spring, usually in May or June. In some families, women did the shearing while in others the husband and wife shared the job. School was sometimes cancelled for the shearing so that the children could help out too. This was particularly true in parts of the country where sheep were grazed and sheared communally. It was a dirty job and women particularly disliked it because of exposure to sheep ticks.

After shearing, the wool was washed in the nearest fast-moving stream. Sometimes this was done by putting it into bags and weighing them down in the water. This cold water wash removed most of the worst dirt and debris but still left a considerable amount of lanolin in the wool. It was then hung on a fence or spread on bushes to dry. Any remaining twigs and foreign matter had to be picked out of the wool before it could be carded. It took a lot of work to produce a clean fleece.

Women diarists often mention working with wool. On September 16, 1815, Louisa Collins, a young Nova Scotia woman, listed her accomplishments and thoughts for the day in her diary. Spinning and knitting were among them and important enough to be recorded.

It is Saturday to day and as usial cleaning house — after that was over I went to spinning, and spun a large ball...I have been sitting by the kitchin fire, knitting this evening; I am preparing for winter — for he approaches very fast, wich prospict then how hopeless — we find the fire side the only cheerful companion, when keen blows the north blast and heavy drives the snow. [56]

After the wool was spun, it was plied together, put in hanks, and washed carefully in preparation for dyeing. Not all wool was dyed. Yarn for working knits was usually kept in its natural shades, but fancier yarns were dyed.

Dyes were made from mundane household ingredients. Many families, especially those of Scottish origin, saved urine as a source of ammonia. This made dye pot concoctions rather lively. Malcolm Foster, a Nova Scotia storyteller who lived in the Annapolis Valley at the turn of the century, recounted an amusing incident where a noisesome dyepot was instrumental in securing a proposal of marriage.

Malcolm was courting a certain young lady in the kitchen of her boarding house one winter night, when things began to happen.

Well, sir, Mrs. Dick had a jeesly big graniteware thundermug on the stove with urine in it. She was brewing some of that old-time dye that they used to make out of elderberries and otherwise worthless ingredients. I think probably she had overslept or forgotten it, and came out in her nighty to have a look at it when she heard my sleigh bells, and then hustled back out of sight. There was a roaring fire on and the darn thing had just about boiled dry; and the air, according to my way of thinking, was getting middling ripe.

Then in a minute or two, the enamel began to "ping," and to fly in all directions of the compass. She was laying down a moderately heavy barrage all over the kitchen...I could see that this situation couldn't last very much longer. For a few more seconds we managed to keep our faces straight. Finally, however, when a big hunk of red-hot enamel let go with a "zing" and sailed past my right ear, I concluded that the time had come for action of some sort.[57]

Malcolm proposed, the young lady accepted him, and they lived happily ever after.

The labour of wool processing and the hazards of home dyeing being what they were, Canadians opened their arms to woollen mills when they became established in their communities, and they were established in great numbers.

Today's Wool

Many knitters believe that there is no fibre better adapted to knitting than pure wool. Although scientists have produced some excellent synthetic fibres, they have not been able to produce a synthetic fibre with the same specific attributes as wool.

Canada is well suited to wool production and, on the whole, it has been a profitable business. However, over the years wool production has declined to a fraction of what it once was. Agriculture Canada tells us that in 1920, 5.1 million kilograms of shorn wool were produced in Canada. The high point in production was in 1945 when almost 7 million kilograms were produced. The low point was in 1976 when production had declined to 1.2 million kilograms.

The prices paid to wool growers are part of the reason why interest in wool production has fluctuated over the years. In 1918, the average price per kilogram of clean, shorn wool was $1.36. In 1932, a dismal year in which nobody was paid much for anything anywhere in the world, the price plummeted to $0.11 per kilogram. The high point in recent years came in 1977 when prices rose to $1.78 per kilogram. Wool farmers do not often become wealthy.

There are signs of a renewed interest in sheep and wool production in Canada. Many farmers raise sheep on a small scale because of interest in the animals themselves and in practising an agricultural lifestyle that may run in their blood. Crusty radio broadcaster Jack Webster, now retired, raises sheep on one of British Columbia's idyllic Gulf Islands. Few Canadians realize too that sheep farming was the family business of the late, lamented culinary queen, Madame Benoit. She and her husband raised sheep on their farm, suitably named Noirmouton, near Sutton, Quebec.

Canadian Cooperative Wool Growers

Before 1914, Canadian wool was not marketed by plan. Many people grew their own wool and knitters with no personal source of supply bought it from individual dealers, junk merchants, traders, and even butchers who acted as middlemen between farmers and consumers.

To improve things, the Canadian government established a special commission to investigate the industry. The commission's recommendations resulted in a system for grading wool. The commission also recommended that Canadian wool be marketed on cooperative lines. By 1916, twenty-six different associations had sprung up to handle the wool clip. In 1918, the Canadian Cooperative Wool Growers Limited was incorporated to organize the marketing effort.

The specific purpose of this organization, which still thrives today, was to promote the well being of the Canadian wool industry by ensuring proper grading to obtain the highest market price and improving the product through proper care and preparation.

Today, about sixty to eighty percent of the annual Canadian wool clip is consigned to the Canadian Cooperative Wool Growers for sale. The organization, with headquarters in Carleton Place, Ontario, near the nation's capital, carries on comprehensive programmes to improve the quality of Canadian fleece.

It operates wool collection outlets in most provinces as well as retail outlets that sell yarn, wool fabrics, sheep-skin products, and stockman's supplies. These shops are a wool lover's paradise, selling everything from mattress pads to posters and attention getting bumper stickers with messages like, "You've never lived till you've lived with a Sheepherder."

Canadian wool is grown in a cold, spacious environment, giving it heightened lustre, whiteness, and elasticity. These positive qualities have created an international market for it, recently attracting the attention of Japanese buyers. In 1989, Mitsui began full-fledged marketing under the logo "Canadian Legend," using the wool's springiness and fine colour as selling points. The Canadian wool will be used to make fabrics, knits, yarn, futons, and other products.

The Wool Bureau of Canada

Much of the wool that goes into hand-knitting yarn in Canada does not come from Canada but from the Southern Hemisphere. The Wool Bureau of Canada, the Canadian Branch of the International Wool Secretariat, promotes the use of Southern Hemisphere wool in Canada and acts as an international standard. Its mandate is to increase the Canadian consumption of wool from the Southern Hemisphere.

Throughout the world, the International Wool Secretariat conducts stringent quality control tests on Woolmark products to ensure a high level of product performance. The tests are for fibre content, abrasion resistance, resistance to "pilling," fabric strength, and colour fastness.

The Woolmark Symbol

It was the IWS that launched the Woolmark scheme in 1964. The Woolmark, one of the world's best recognized trademarks, certifies that products are made from one hundred percent pure new (virgin) wool. Virgin wool is wool that has never been used before, not simply reprocessed wool. The products include clothing, carpets, home furnishings, blankets, and hand-knitting yarn. Only products made by licensed manufacturers, according to strict international standards, can qualify for the distinctive Woolmark label.

The Woolmark symbol was designed by an Italian, Francesco Saroglia. He was one of thirteen international designers who worked on ideas for the Woolmark. An international panel of seven design experts chose Saroglia's sketch after studying eighty-six possible designs.

Saroglia wanted to suggest wool yarn in the structure of his design, and he began by twisting and bending strips of paper marked with black and white lines. By chance, he caught sight of one of the designs reflected in glass; the curve of the black and white lines bent abruptly to a sharper angle where they touched the glass surface. He started to sketch, and the Woolmark was born.

Today, the Woolmark symbol is recognized and understood by more than four hundred million consumers around the world. It is the best-known textile trademark in the world.

Innovations in Wool Processing

Wool's most marvellous properties — its warmth, its elasticity, and its ability to absorb dye — make it a joy to work with. Its susceptibility to moths and to shrinkage can make it a heartbreak.

Over the years, many dedicated scientists have worked to improve the performance of wool in these respects, and the pages of Canadian knitting pattern books echo the names of their inventions. "Patonizing," "Kroy processing," "MITIN mothproofing," and "superwash wool" are some of the terms familiar to Canadian knitters. What do they mean and where did they come from?

"Patonizing" was the name given by Patons & Baldwins to the process it developed in Britain in the 1940s to make wool yarns shrink resistant. Like most other processes, it was based on the chemical modification (by chlorination) of the surface of the wool fibre to reduce the microscopic scaliness that causes a wool fabric to shrink when washed. The process is no longer used in Canada where "Kroy" is more popular.

"Kroy" is the name given by Kroy Unshrinkable Wools Limited to a similar process it developed in Canada around the same time. This process, which is applicable to combed wool sliver rather than yarn, was vastly improved in the 1970s when Kroy Unshrinkable Wools Limited introduced its patented "deep immersion" technique, which it now licenses worldwide.

Kroy Unshrinkable Wools Limited was founded in 1944. The parent company was York Knitting Mills Ltd., and the name "Kroy" was coined by spelling "York" backwards. The name quickly became known to Canadians, and today it is a trademark that is registered and recognized in most major wool using countries.

The original process was purchased from a Scotsman by the name of John McLauchlan but had to be upgraded quickly by Kroy chemists to meet the Canadian demand for complete washability. Kroy now has three technologies that it licenses around the world for the treatment of wool top, loose wool, and wool fabric.

"MITIN" is the name given by Ciba Geigy, the Swiss chemical company, for its treatment that protects wool from keratin-eating insects. The mothproof and beetleproof finishes stay in place during dry cleaning, washing, and when exposed to light. There is no odour and no impairment of the handle or appearance of the wool.

"Superwash" is a standard developed by the International Wool Secretariat to determine a woven or knitted fabric's resistance to shrinkage through either machine washing or machine drying. The "superwash" treatment involves coating each wool fibre with a miniscule amount of resin. This coating allows the fibres to rub against each other during machine washing without their scales becoming interlocked. It cannot be washed out of the garment.

Wool is so valuable and its properties so unique that no expense has been spared to improve on nature's endowment and to bring Canadians pure wool yarns of the first quality.

Nylon: Canada's First Synthetic Knitting Yarn

The development of synthetic yarns revolutionized yarn production in Canada. The fibre responsible for the breakthrough was nylon. The technology for producing nylon was perfected during World War II, but it was not until the 1950s that it became widely available on the consumer market. The *New Lux Knitting Book*, 1951 edition, announced the development in glowing terms.

New...and NEWS! That's nylon yarn! Born in a test tube, nylon now takes its place in the knitting field — a development which will be welcomed eagerly by every woman who knits.

Nylon yarns became available in Canada less than a year ago, and as a result, most wool manufacturers are still experimenting with various combinations of nylon and wool, as well as with pure nylon yarns. Most of us know by now the special properties of nylon. However, to mention some of the most important features, it has great tensile strength, is shrinkproof, wears well, and is easy to wash and dry. These properties are invaluable, particularly for children's clothes....

The newest type of nylon yarn has what is known as a permanent crimp — a special process which enables the yarn to retain its shape after washing, as well as making it softer and more pliable. At the present time nylon yarn is being made only in one weight — equivalent to three ply wool....

The rest is history. Synthetic yarns have improved greatly since those early days and are now available in every weight, colour, and texture. Some are blended with other fibres to produce a full range of effects for knitters to enjoy. Soft mohairs, cotton looks, chenilles, and Shetland tweeds can all be made from high quality synthet-ics. Knitters often compliment synthetic yarns by saying, "it looks just like the real thing!" They are the most popular yarns in Canada today.

Commercial Yarn Producers

Patons & Baldwins in Canada

The recent history of Canadian knitting could not be written without Patons & Baldwins. Its products have made an indelible impression on the minds and memories of Canadian knitters. Its name is familiar to many non-knitters as well for Patons & Baldwins has supplied us with yarn, with pattern books, with ideas, and with encouragement through all the years of this century, and it gives every indication of being the dominant force in Canadian hand-knitting yarns in the next. How did the company get its start?

Mr. James Baldwin (1746–1811) of Halifax, England, and Mr. John Paton (1768–1848) of Alloa, Scotland, never met one another. In fact, there is a strong likelihood that they would react with extreme horror to the pairing of their names, for the two companies did not amalgamate until 1920. In their own lifetimes and through three generations of both families, they were the greatest of commercial rivals. They built two empires that competed with one another for market share in Britain's developing textile industry. They were vigorous competitors and in the early "no holds barred" years of the Industrial Revolution, competition was vigorous indeed.

Despite the rivalry of their firms, James Baldwin and John Paton were energetic entrepreneurs who had a great deal in common. Baldwin's first business was a wool washing and cloth fulling concern, which he established in 1785. He later expanded it to include carding, dyeing, and worsted spinning operations. In his lifetime, he was his firm's only salesman and he travelled the length of England and Scotland selling his yarns. English knitting historian Michael Harvey wrote that "he was a strong patriarchal figure, being referred to as 'Father' by all members of his family."

In 1813, John Paton founded his firm, twenty-eight years after Mr. Baldwin. He began business with a machine spinning concern, something that was rather rare in the Scotland of his time where hand spinning still predominated. He later expanded his firm to include a dye works.

Both men were frugal and, in common with most hard-driving entrepreneurs, they immediately re-invested their profits in the early years. Both men took family members into their firms, ensuring continuity of leadership in the years to come.

Mr. Baldwin, "who kept a good cellar," died at the age of sixty-five. Mr. Paton, a religious man who was "temperate," died at the age of eighty. Both died knowing they had accomplished something.

The continuing success of both firms depended on sound commercial judgement and on keeping an eye open for opportunities. Both became megafirms that maintained good relations with their workers and a sense of community responsibility. The great resurgence of knitting as a leisure-time pursuit during the reign of Queen Victoria fuelled their growth.

Expansion came quickly. In 1861, Patons had one hundred and fifty employees. By 1872, the year in which the production of "fingering" yarn began, there were four hundred and fifty. Such spectacular growth meant that the local wool supply could no longer fill the needs of these burgeoning megafirms. At first, they purchased wool from other parts of Britain, until this supply was exhausted too. Finally, Patons took the adventurous step of sending its wool buyer to Australia to acquire wool directly. Patons' excellent supply of wool became a considerable competitive advantage in the years to come. Baldwins buyers also bought wool in Australia and then in South Africa, Argentina, and Spain.

Protecting a business advantage once gained is the other side of the entrepreneurial coin. Both firms had adopted graphic symbols to distinguish their yarns from those of their competitors when they first began to grow. The passing of the Trade Marks Act in 1875 produced a rash of registrations of these symbols, which had been in use for many years. Patons adopted the "Rose and hand" symbol and the motto *virtute viget*, "it thrives by goodness." The "Paton's rose" was registered on April 29, 1885. In September 1888, Patons also registered the "White heather and bonnet" device.

Baldwins had already registered its trademark, a beehive, on May 3, 1876. The beehive was later chosen as the logo of the merged firm of Patons & Baldwins and eventually became one of the world's best-recognized symbols. Seldom has a corporate logo been more effective. In a piece of remarkable understatement, the registration documents noted that "there was no part of the civilised world in which it was not known and appreciated."

The business climate that developed in Britain after World War I made industry consolidation inevitable. The merger of the two firms came in April 1920, and it must have rocked the knitting world. At the time of its formation, the new combined company had more than eleven mills and seven agencies in four countries. The Halifax mills of the Baldwin company eventually disappeared, and the head office of Patons & Baldwins today is in Darlington. The firm's production facilities are on the site of the original mill in Alloa. At present, Patons & Baldwins Ltd. has the largest hand-knitting yarn manufacturing capacity in the United Kingdom with twenty-five percent of all production being exported.

The old firm of John Paton, Son & Co. had a warehouse in Montreal and a general agency in Vancouver before the merger of 1920. Baldwins also had a clientele in "the Dominions," but nobody knows precisely when its Canadian involvement began.

We do know that Patons did an active business selling yarn through Eaton's catalogue, dating from the turn of the century. The first catalogue was published in 1884 so this underlines Patons responsiveness in recognizing a good opportunity when it saw one. The mail-order sales strategy virtually guaranteed market penetration in a thinly populated country, where mounting an effective retail operation was rather difficult. The vast distances in many parts of Canada made opportunities for personal shopping few and far between so Canadians were deeply attached to their mail-order catalogues.

The merger of Patons & Baldwins in Britain cleared the way for foreign expansion. The first mill established outside Britain was built in Tasmania in 1923, and then the company turned its eyes to Canada. It originally selected Vancouver for its base of operations and its agent there was Duncan Carmichael, a man much celebrated in inner corporate circles. The British Columbia agency maintained close ties with England until the end of World War II. But because of Vancouver's distance from other major population centres in Canada, a need for a more central base of operations was recognized.

Michael Harvey, who wrote the official history of the parent company for its bicentennial in 1985, casts some interesting light on the firm's beginnings in Toronto.

Thomas O. Aked emigrated from Yorkshire to Canada in 1909 as a salesman for an English woollen firm. He later became manager for the Monarch Knitting Company.

In 1918, he formed Aked and Company Ltd. and had a factory in Toronto, which produced fancy hand-knitting yarns. Harvey tells us that Thomas Aked is credited with having wound the first ball of knitting wool made in Canada. He also invented an improved spinning machine, the Aked Prince Smith Flyer Doffer, thus ensuring the success and growth of his business.

Acquiring a successful operating business was a logical way for Patons & Baldwins to establish a physical presence in Canada, and it acquired the Aked firm in 1928. Growing demand for its products necessitated larger premises, and in 1931 Patons & Baldwins built the Toronto mill that it still occupies. Early photographs show the mill rising up out of a splendid rural countryside; a countryside that is today considered to be very nearly downtown Toronto. At first, the isolation was a matter of some concern. How would the firm attract workers when it was so far out of town? This did not worry the builders one bit. The fact that the mill was built close to a railway line was a great deal more important, and they were right.

For many years, Patons & Baldwins was a British company that carried on business in Canada, but in 1963, Patons & Baldwins Canada was incorporated. Patons & Baldwins continues to sell some of its British yarns here today, but the greatest part of its business and its continuing success comes from producing yarns and patterns for Canadians. Its finely tuned design department knows how to capture the Canadian imagination and to keep us knitting with its yarns year after year. After all, as one early pattern book expressed it:

Across the country East and West
You hear wise knitters say with zest —
"The wools we like the very best
Are Beehive."

Spinrite Yarns and Dyers

Canadian entrepreneurs hold their own when it comes to recognizing an opportunity and taking advantage of it. Such an entrepreneur was David D. Hay, the man who made Spinrite Yarns what it is today — one of the most diversified manufacturers of knitting yarns in North America. Its yarns are marketed under the recognized and respected name of Bouquet.

Spinrite Yarns had its beginnings in 1913, before the time of David Hay, and its story tells a lot about the vigorous pioneer spirit that characterized our country well into our own times.

One day in 1913, Mr. Max Becker, a German immigrant and qualified machine knitter, was on his way by train to Kincardine, Ontario, with the intention of establishing a knitwear plant. He never arrived. On the train, he met a man from Listowel, Ontario, named Aaron Ringler. When Ringler heard of Becker's plan, he persuaded him to stop off in Listowel and to consider opening his plant there. History is full of such fortuitous accidents.

The town of Listowel was first known as Mapleton but was later renamed for a town in County Kerry, Ireland. It was incorporated as a village in 1866 and had achieved town status by 1874. A prosperous place, one of its early shop-keepers was John Livingstone, brother of the famous Dr. David Livingstone, the African explorer and missionary. These interesting factors were probably less important in Becker's decision to stop off than was the fact that Listowel had an abundant supply of fresh water and railway connections with the wider world.

With the financial help of several citizens and five thousand dollars, Perfect Knitting Mills was established in 1913, the name setting the tone for its standard of performance. Its first product was machine-knit sweaters, and during World War I there was a great demand for Perfect Knit Sweaters by the army. (Spinrite Yarns continues to supply woollen sweaters to the Canadian armed forces today.)

About 1916, the company expanded and built a spinning and dyeing mill on the location of the present plant in central Listowel. Expansion following the war meant the addition of new buildings. The great expense, coupled with an economic downturn placed Perfect Knitting Mills on the verge of bankruptcy in 1924.

Quick financing saved the company but made it vulnerable, and in 1931, Perfect Knitting Mills was sold to a Hamilton, Ontario, concern and renamed Maitland Spinning Mills Ltd. The company prospered until 1952, when a sharp recession in the textile industry resulted in the decision to close the plant in Listowel.

Mr. David Hay, a native of Listowel and the descendant of an early immigrant from Aberdeen, Scotland, had joined the company in 1926. He had learned the dyeing trade and eventually became head dyer for the firm. In 1948, he left Listowel to take up a position as Canadian General Manager of the Geigy company, later known as Ciba Geigy.

When the mill came up for sale in 1952, he returned to his hometown and formed the company today known as Spinrite. It was a rescue with

Early days at Spinrite Yarns and Dyers, Listowel, Ontario

great personal significance because it allowed Hay to make a real contribution to the community that had helped his ancestors to prosper. Under Hay's direction, operations started on a small scale during the early troubled times for the textile industry, but the mill prospered and began to be well known in Canada.

When Mary Maxim sweaters became popular in the 1950s, Spinrite pioneered the development of its heavy "homespun" type of knitting yarn, and Northland yarn is still made there today. Spinrite then began to make different types and weights of knitting yarn for Mary Maxim, who remains a good customer, and to increase production of its own brands, which the Canadian public buys in great quantities.

The large and thoroughly modern Spinrite plant is a showpiece for the latest in yarn technology. It contains both a worsted and a woollen mill, a scouring operation, and a dye house. It produces large quantities of yarn for the machine knitwear industry as well as a wide variety of hand knitting yarns of different fibres and blends.

David Hay died in 1985, but his shrewd eye for opportunity and his legacy of responsiveness to changing conditions remains. His work is carried on by his two sons Robert and Douglas and by the entire Spinrite team.

White Buffalo Mills

Western knitters are a breed apart. They know what they want in knitting yarns and when they find it they support it.

This has been the experience of White Buffalo Mills of Brandon, Manitoba, a business that began to capture the interest of western knitters in the late 1950s.

Today's White Buffalo Mills became a company in 1979, but its roots go much deeper. The heart of the woollen mill itself is more than eighty years old, although some new sections have been added over the years. Situated on the historic Assiniboine River, it was originally a lumber mill, but the business changed and it has produced hand-knitting yarns for more than thirty years. White Buffalo was formerly known as Metev Woolen Mills and prior to that as Brandon Woolen Mills.

The mill operates on the woollen system of processing, and in its early years it mainly produced blankets from scrap woollens brought in by the public for re-processing. Sometime in the late 1960s, Mr. Metev, the owner of the mill at the time, saw British Columbia Indians knitting garments from unspun wool that they carded by hand. Metev determined that the machinery in his mill could produce this yarn and save labour. White Buffalo Unspun yarn was born. He patented the process immediately. Today's Unspun is six strands of carded wool, but in earlier years custom manufacturing provided customers with single-strand and four-strand versions of its yarn.

As market demand increased in British Columbia and moved into Alberta and the prairies, a distribution network was developed. Department store chains began to carry unspun and its popularity was enormous. The distinctive "cakes" of yarn were everywhere in knitters' homes. When western knitters thought of woollen yarn, they thought of White Buffalo before anything else.

Other products were soon added to the company's line. Elena (once known as Elenka) yarn was in great demand for knitting heavy Icelandic sweaters, and White Buffalo began to market its products aggressively. Over the years, some blends of synthetic and pure wool have been developed to satisfy the taste for easy care yarns.

In the 1980s, White Buffalo actively encouraged its design and pattern production department, and even sponsored a national design contest that had excellent results and boosted its image across Canada. White Buffalo has produced close to one hundred original sweater designs that show a strong native Indian influence. These uniquely Canadian designs, still popular today, use birds, whales, and other motifs from the natural world as their chief inspiration. Knitting a White Buffalo sweater is like knitting a piece of the Canadian West with history and life in every stitch. With proper care, each garment should last at least twenty years.

Westerners have remained enthusiastically loyal to their very own brand of yarn, but White Buffalo also has a broad North American distribution base. Its yarns are unique knitting treasures that reflect Canadian tastes and Canadian ways.

Briggs & Little Woolen Mills

In 1857, ten years before Confederation, there was a mill on the Magaguadavic River near Harvey Station, New Brunswick. There is still a mill there today. Briggs & Little Woolen Mills has survived changing leisure-time interests and fashion trends, competition from synthetic yarns, and a competitive business environment that would make weaker willed people quit.

Roots run deep in the Maritime provinces and business histories are as complicated as family relationships. The names of the first owners of this mill are no longer remembered, but by 1910, it was owned by Roy and Alex Little and a Mr. Coburn. In 1913, the business became known as Little's Woolen Mill. In 1916, Matthew Briggs paired up with members of the Little family, and the company assumed the name that generations of knitters have known so well. Today's owners of the firm are descendents of those original enterprising people, and wool seems to run in their blood.

Maritime knitters have used Briggs & Little 100% pure wool yarn for as long as they and their grandparents can remember. Four generations of my family have knit with it, and Briggs & Little yarn was used in a knitting duel staged by two of my great grandmothers, which I wrote about in Chapter 3.

In the earliest days, the company produced only black, white, and four shades of blended gray yarn. Its range quickly grew, and today the company produces more than sixty colours of yarn in four weights. Some of its most popular shades have been in production for more than forty years. Colours like Briar Rose and Fundy Fog stir up images of soft summer days, and the yarns themselves can be used to paint landscapes in wool. Folk art knitters like Lynn Maclachlan and producers of finished hand-knit sweaters like Nova Scotia's Cumberland County Knitters enjoy Briggs & Little yarns and produce extraordinarily vibrant effects using them.

The Briggs & Little mill itself is a wonder. Three stories tall, it is perched over a deep, wide mill pond. It is full of wool processing equipment that is many years old and is maintained in perfect working order. Water is still used to power some of the machinery in the mill. Reliable machinery and a good supply of water have helped to keep

The mill owned by Amos Little & Son, York Mills, New Brunswick.

Briggs & Little competitive in a time when most people assume that high technology rules the world of business. Moreover, the company is so well known among knitters that customers find Briggs & Little; Briggs & Little is not obliged to find them. Most of its marvellous yarn is sold by mail order, although general stores and yarn outlets in the Atlantic provinces always keep a good supply on hand. It is shipped everywhere in Canada and to many places in the United States where knitters appreciate pure wool.

Briggs & Little's location is historic, its premises are historic, and its yarns are historic, but it is a history that satisfies a modern need for beauty and quality. Before Canada was a country, Briggs & Little was a woollen mill.

Farmers Who Make Yarn

Since the Industrial Revolution set the model for manufacturing operations in the world, the trend in the business of producing knitting yarns has been to ever bigger companies that satisfy ever larger markets.

This does not sit well with everybody. Some people do not picture themselves running mills or sitting behind desks, even though both are essential to supplying Canada with quality knitting yarns. They want to operate their own farms, be their own masters, live where they want to live, and make beautiful yarns on a scale that they can personally manage.

These are the gourmets of the yarn production business, people who are personally involved with every skein of yarn sold to a knitter. Their businesses are not big, but they are influential and they supply the discerning knitter with something unique and precious.

Canada has hundreds of small-scale, "boutique" yarn producers, as we might call them, living lives of quiet satisfaction and great usefulness. Eugene Bourgeois and Barbara Morrow are but two whose businesses give us a glimpse of the lives of farmers who make yarn. Thanks to appreciative knitters, some of them have become very well known indeed.

Philosopher's Wool

Eugene Bourgeois, The Philosopher Shepherd, is a sheep farmer who wanted to help other sheep farmers. But back in 1976, he was still working on a doctorate in philosophy and had no intention of farming at all. He believes that his background in philosophy taught him to think independently and to never take "no" for an answer.

Eugene, his school librarian wife Ann, and their three children moved to a small farm near Inverhuron, Ontario, where they began to raise sheep quite accidentally. Their first sheep was a gift from a friend whom they had helped at lambing time. Others were added and their flock began to grow.

The philosopher got quite a shock when he sold his first clip of wool and found out how low market prices were. He could not understand why farmers should receive so little of the selling price of finished yarn. Rather than simply accept the situation graciously, in 1985 he formed the Philosopher's Wool Company and sent off fifty pounds of raw wool for processing.

He sold the finished yarn to friends and by word of mouth and improved his return considerably. Knitters loved the yarn, which kept much of its natural oiliness, and they made beautiful sweaters from it. They also wanted more. Eugene began to buy the fleece of other farmers who were too uninvolved to sell it themselves. He was able to pay them more than the going rate. "Bring our shepherds in from the cold" read one of his slogans, and that is exactly what he did.

Today, Philosopher's Wool is a flourishing business that has grown far beyond the original concept of getting the best price for raw wool. Ann Bourgeois, the philosopher's wife, is a talented knitter. She designed some magnificent sweaters using their own yarns, and the company began to supply these unique designs in kit form. When some customers asked for finished sweaters, they organized a network of home knitters who now keep very busy filling orders for Philosopher's Wool.

Retailing has changed too. Where once the shepherd and his family sold their wool by word of mouth, they now sell it in stores, at craft shows, by mail, and in their own retail outlet, The Philosopher's Stone, a place where wool has been turned into gold for everybody concerned.

Prosperity and success have not corrupted Eugene's philosophy. He still shares the wealth from his wool with the farmers and knitters who work with him. As the Philosopher's Wool motto appropriately puts it, what is "good for ewe is good for us all."

Willow Bend Farm

Barbara Morrow, the owner of Willow Bend Farm, near London, Ontario, is a sheep breeder and a true artisan with her yarns. She has been raising sheep for nearly thirty years and continues to discover the wonderful possibilities of working with her own top-grade wool. She keeps a close eye on her flock, which she can see from the window of her farm house, making certain that the

A curious onlooker stands before the log cabin at Willow Bend Farm.

animals are satisfied and that their fleeces stay clean and in good condition. This is half the battle for any wool farmer. It is a demanding job because her flock at present numbers more than three hundred and includes sheep of different breeds. She is also actively involved in selling breeding stock.

Barbara's father taught her to knit when she was a little girl and he was at home with a serious illness. He was a prize-winning knitter who often won awards for his work in the competitions held at the Canadian National Exhibition in Toronto. Barbara inherited his skill and has a wonderful opportunity to use it at Willow Bend Farm.

Today, Barbara produces her own yarn and custom dyes and paints it in a palette of glorious shades of her own invention. Many knitters dream of colours of yarn that they would like to work with but can never find in stores. When Barbara imagines a colour, she makes it. A few years ago she opened her own wool shop in a restored, 130-year-old log cabin on the farm at Willow Bend.

She also designs, knits, and sells luxurious sweaters that use her own hand-crafted, one of a kind yarns. Each one is a jewel that cannot be imitated using commercial wools. These are the unique pleasures of the farmer who makes yarn.

Luxury Fibres in Canada

When did Canadians first begin to think of using luxury fibres for hand knitting? Silks were used in small quantities, dating from the nineteenth century, but did not become affordable for knitting entire garments. The angora craze of the 1950s may have been the first mass knitting movement that recognized the possibilities of other animal fibres. A few years later, the great fashion knitting awakening of the mid-1980s created a voracious appetite for beautiful and exotic fibres — but then propelled them firmly out of reach of most of our pocketbooks.

Canadian yarn lovers took to their spinning wheels and began to investigate the possibilities of the wider world of fibre. These modern-day yarn pioneers have stopped at nothing to create exotic home-grown yarns. No woolly animal is too unpromising and no labour too great to make yarn from what most knitters can only think of as some very raw, raw materials indeed.

Angora, mohair, and dog hair yarns are now thriving businesses in Canada, and they have expanded our concept of what Canadian knitting yarns can be. Home growers now produce these luxuriant fibres in greater amounts, but they continue to be rare and beautiful hand-processed fibres. Many Canadian knitters have become slaves to their touch.

Candace Angoras

Candace Carter's soft and sensuous yarns come from German angora rabbits. Once she had only four of these fluffy creatures, but happily the rabbits took care of that in their time-honoured way and now she has well over a hundred.

Candace Carter displays her angora yarns at a craft show.

Before she owned any rabbits, Candace was a fine arts student who planned a career in commercial art. At one point in her studies, she realized that she would probably starve as an artist so she decided to study agriculture — to learn how to feed herself, she declares.

In 1983, she combined her artistic and agrarian impulses and began Candace Angoras, hoping to sell ready-made sweaters to fashionable Toronto boutiques. This proved exceptionally difficult. Her home angora production could not support the quantities of yarn needed to supply the wholesale market on a continuing basis. Then, price became a real barrier as retailers added on their percentage. However, the good news was that store owners loved Candace's sweaters.

She wisely decided to sell finished yarn instead and to make her designs available as hand-knitting kits. Today, her product line not only includes kits for small items like gloves and hats but also big, beautiful, luxurious garments like cardigans, jackets, and evening dresses. Many are made from pure angora, but other Candace Carter yarns combine angora with merino, silk, and cotton for strength and beauty. Miraculously, they do not shed.

From such beginnings, Candace also became an authority on the care and feeding of angora rabbits. Along the way she founded the Ontario Angora Producers Association and became its first president. She is a true enthusiast, lavishing care on her rabbits and plucking the raw fibre from each animal by hand. It takes one hour to pluck the hair from one rabbit, and this cannot be done before they are ready to shed.

As a fibre artist and as a farmer, Candace Carter gets an opportunity to work with one of the most luxurious yarns that nature can produce. Canadian knitters get the rewards.

Kaprikid Mohair & Wool

Rhoda and Colin Stone live in the incomparable Peace River country of Alberta. It is an area of vast farms, wide, meandering rivers, and more open air than most city-dwelling Canadians could ever imagine. The huge unspoiled vistas make people think big when it comes to deciding what to do with their lives. The boundaries and fences that other people see are simply not part of the Albertan vision of things.

The Stones began their farming adventure with a simple dairy goat, which they bought when they discovered that their baby daughter was allergic to infant formula. They loved the curious nature and intelligence of goats, but found it hard to be tied to twice daily milkings.

They began their fibre adventure when they saw their first angora goats and were captivated by their charm. One look at these unusual animals with their thick curly fleece makes fibre artists'

fingers itch and a whole new world of tactile possibilities explode in their minds.

Angora goats have a long history of domestication, but until the 1850s they were zealously protected from export by the Turkish government. The United States and South Africa obtained some breeding stock, and huge herds in Texas and South Africa now supply the bulk of the world's mohair.

The Stones started with two bred does and now have a herd of over fifty. They also became interested in sheep, and after experimenting with several breeds have decided that Polypays are best suited to their operation. Mohair is a long, soft, silky fibre. Compared to wool, it is warmer, stronger, and more lustrous but wool is more elastic. A blend of the two fibres makes a superior yarn.

Rhoda Stone of Kaprikid Mohair & Wool with two of her young angora goats.

Rhoda began by washing, carding, and spinning her own wool and mohair, but the herd grew too quickly to continue on this scale. Now she has their Country Treasures yarn commercially spun but hand dyes it personally. A blend of fifty percent mohair and fifty percent wool, Rhoda has created a range of shades that express their Alberta life — close to home and close to nature. Delicious colours like "fresh cream," "ripe wheat," "wild rose," and "wide sky" evoke the beauty of the prairie landscape in the minds of receptive knitters. They also cause the tastebuds to tingle.

Kaprikid Mohair & Wool sells yarn and sweater kits by mail. Rhoda also does custom knitting and designing. She sells her sweaters personally to lucky customers and at Handspirits, a superb Calgary retail shop. Rhoda has always enjoyed knitting, but it is special to her now. The Stone's life is full of the meaning one gets from living and working in one of Canada's unique beauty spots.

Gone to the Dogs in the Yukon

The Canadian knitting life has many faces.

Some knitters make a quick trip to the yarn shop, select a pattern and some yarn, return home, and then begin knitting. Claudia MacPhee, who lives in the woods near Tagish, Yukon, does it differently. She collects the hair her sled dogs shed, spins and dyes it, and then knits it into works of art that are worn around the world. Hers is a unique Canadian knitting story.

Claudia's grandmother taught her to knit when she was a little girl. She also taught her to take pride in her workmanship and to construct garments without relying on patterns. Young Claudia learned to fit a sock to a foot, a hat to a head, and a sweater to a body, guided by traditional knitting principles. Her grandmother's patient and exacting instruction gave her a mastery of classical technique and the independent mind that has ruled her choice of lifestyle and work.

She later taught herself to spin wool and to weave, and made her living as a weaver for several years. In 1972, she and her husband moved further north. They were too far away from urban centres to continue doing business with retail outlets in southern British Columbia so she started knitting and sold her homespun mittens in the North. They proved to be wonderful sellers, and gradually Claudia's looms became dust catchers and her needles took up the slack.

At the same time, she got her dog team together, something she had always wanted to do. When the dogs shed their coats in the spring, she began to spin the hair into yarn. She liked the

result so she made up some mitts and hats. Their impact was immediate and they sold very quickly.

By 1980, Claudia was tired of working in natural colours and needed a new artistic direction. She experimented with dyeing the dog hair. Owners of the shops that sold her work were not amused, so it was a big surprise to everybody when sales of her new colourful knits skyrocketed. Claudia began to have fun again.

The media soon discovered the winding path to her unusual door and dog fur knits became a Yukon item. Despite the fact that she has never advertised, her many radio broadcasts, TV appearances, and satisfied customers have brought her worldwide fame. The North is a particular haven for European tourists these days. They love its rugged beauty and refreshing life. A German man once turned up at Claudia's home to buy a sweater. He had heard about her in Grise Fjord, a settlement on the southern tip of Ellesmere Island.

Claudia MacPhee of Tagish, Yukon, spins the hair of her sled dogs in her studio.

Many of Claudia's sweaters leave the country on the backs of tourists and foreign visitors, but local people love them too. Political leader Audrey McLaughlin is often seen wearing a Claudia MacPhee creation in the House of Commons.

Claudia has met many customers through dog mushing. They also help to supply her with fibre, and she needs all the dog hair that she can get to fuel her forty- to sixty-hour knitting week. Local dog team owners and groomers save hair for her and donations are always welcome. The best breeds for spinning are those with long under-coats like long-haired Malamute, Samoyed, Golden Retriever, and some Collies. Dogs in the Yukon are inclined to follow the laws of nature rather than the imperatives of pedigree, and some of the more spectacular cross breeds provide the most interesting yarns. Claudia has had great results from the hair of Newfoundland-Malamute and Collie-Samoyed crosses.

Claudia never takes a holiday from knitting. She keeps at her job year round, but in the glorious Northern summer she takes time to tie fishing flies, to garden, and to raise rabbits and chickens. Their summer garden produces the year's vegetables for her husband, herself, and their four children. She also grows more than sixty-five kinds of flowers that are her pride and joy and the source of much artistic inspiration for her vivid sweaters. Her flowers, her dogs, the Yukon's long summer twilight, and the freshness of her world are perpetual sources of pleasure that find their way into her uniquely Canadian work.

Qiviuq: The Great Northern Fibre

Canada's Arctic regions are a rich and fertile place. But few people know that Canada's North is also the home of one of the world's most exotic fibre treasures. Finer than cashmere and warmer than wool, it is qiviuq, the under-down of the musk ox. The word "qiviuq" (pronounced KIV-ee-uk) means "down" in the language of the Inuvialuit people of the Western Arctic. It has also been spelled "qiviut" or even "kiviuk." Like cashmere, vicuna, and camel hair, it is technically a hair, not a wool.

The coat of the musk ox has two distinct layers, a heavy, shaggy outer layer full of coarse guard hairs and a thick, light undercoat of qiviuq. The two layers provide effective insulation that not only protects the animals from the most severe cold but also lessens their food requirements so that they can live on the sparse forage found in the Arctic much of the year.

Musk oxen shed their coat every spring, and it blows across the tundra, collecting in hollows and catching up on twigs and plants. A mature male animal sheds about six pounds of qiviuq each season. There have been attempts to domesticate musk oxen, but the largest world population of these mighty and ancient animals roams free in the Canadian Arctic.

Qiviuq has a long history, but it only became commercially available to hand knitters in the 1980s. Developing both the potential of the fibre and the market for it is largely the work of one woman named Wendy Chambers. Her company, Down North, located in Whitehorse, has turned this rare, wild fibre into some of the most spectacular hand-knitting yarn the world has ever seen.

The first non-native to take note of qiviuq and to appreciate its potential was a Hudson Bay Company trader named Nicholas Jérémie, who spent the years between 1694 and 1714 at York Factory. Jérémie found some of the loose down, and it intrigued him so much that in 1708 he had a pair of stockings made from quivuq. They were made in France and were said to be finer than silk.

Seeing and appreciating qiviuq was one thing, but collecting it was another. Few people bothered, but in the early decades of the twentieth century Norwegian sealers spoke of collecting musk ox down in Greenland for their wives to spin and make into scarves, mittens, and gloves.

While wintering on Melville Island in 1917, Vilhjalmur Stefansson sent a sample of musk ox fibre to Sir Robert Borden in Ottawa. His letter to Borden concluded:

I most sincerely believe that musk oxen can make a square mile of the arctic tundra as valuable as sheep can a square mile of Alberta.[58]

Stefansson spent the next forty years pursuing plans for a musk ox domestication scheme that would create Arctic wealth, but it never caught fire. While he was commander of the Canadian Arctic Expedition (1913–1918), he collected sixty pounds of raw fibre and had some of it made into socks and mittens. Some fibre was also sent to Leeds University in England for extensive testing to determine its properties.

These tests were carried out in 1922. Textile experts compared it with eight other animal fibres and found that it compared favourably with the finest cashmere or vicuna. However, the importance of first separating the coarse guard hairs from the soft under-down was not fully understood for many years, and the test team found it rather difficult to card and spin. They concluded their report by suggesting that if the material could be procured in fair weights, there would be a market for it in knitted goods and that it seemed to be more suitable for knitting than for weaving. More than sixty years later Wendy Chambers proved them right.

Further tests in 1932 confirmed the fineness of the fibre, but European and Canadian interests in the commercial exploitation of qiviuq waned because of the difficulties involved.

Textile enthusiasts in Alaska remained especially interested and in the following decades many small-scale experiments and projects were conducted. In the 1930s, the making of qiviuq scarves was a rage among Alaskan co-eds. In the 1970s, Lillian Crowell Schell did excellent work organizing a knitting project with Alaskan native women. Experience with the fibre grew slowly and because of the interest in Alaska, appreciation of qiviuq did not die. To see and touch qiviuq is to love it; it will always have loyal followers.

Wendy Chambers and Down North

Wendy Chambers is a spinner, knitter, and weaver who has always had a particular feeling for fine specialty fibres. Down North is Canada's only commercial supplier of precious qiviuq knitting yarns marketed under the name Polar Seas.

Growing up and living in British Columbia, Wendy heard occasional rumours about this miracle fibre, but it was several years before she found a sample to work with. Wendy moved to Whitehorse in the late 1970s and was then able to use her northern location as a base for her intensive work with qiviuq.

One of Wendy's first interests was encouraging the harvesting of raw qiviuq and ensuring its supply, work that already took her one step beyond what Stefansson had been able to achieve. She began travelling to places in the western Arctic and working with native women to locate qiviuq and to prepare it for processing.

As Wendy's personal experience with qiviuq deepened, she began to perfect ways of handling it to bring out its superb qualities and to teach others her skills.

The Sachs Harbour Qiviuq Project was one of the earliest formal teaching endeavours. Sachs Harbour is a tiny settlement on Banks Island, the home of the world's largest concentration of musk oxen. The project was organized by Jackie Kuptana, a local woman who wanted the women of

Sachs Harbour to utilize and benefit economically from this renewable resource found on their doorstep. Workshop courses taught the spinning and dyeing of qiviuq, using natural dyes made from Arctic lichen. A later workshop, organized by Sheila McDonnell, manager of the Ikahuk Co-op, focussed on knitting skills. Wendy Chambers was the project instructor. Today, several women on Banks Island derive income from harvesting qiviuq or from spinning and knitting with qiviuq yarn.

A Northern woman holds her first skein of qiviuq yarn, spun during the Sachs Harbour Qiviuq Project.

In cooperation with the Holman Eskimo Cooperative in the hamlet of Holman on Victoria Island, Wendy began conducting qiviuq workshops for fibre enthusiasts from other parts of Canada and from all around the world. Every July for the past five years, a different group has gathered in Holman to spend a week working with qiviuq — on its native tundra in the middle of the spectacular Arctic summer.

In its raw form, qiviuq is a fluffy, ash-coloured down of incredible lightness and softness, but it is

The Challenge
of the Mountains

An early CPR brochure extolled
the outdoor life in Canada.
This young lady's hand knits
have Scottish roots.

The author, sometimes known as "Shirl the Purl," in her studio.

Participants at the 1989 Arctic Experience for Fiberists workshop held in Holman, N.W.T.

a long way from being usable as knitting yarn.

After much exploration, Wendy found a mill that would de-hair qiviuq mechanically, and then spin it to gossamer fineness. Because of its remarkable softness, it has little shape retention and a garment knit with pure qiviuq yarn would not drape well. Wendy plies the spun qiviuq with a fine merino wool before dyeing it. The merino provides strength and elasticity and takes a brighter dye than the darker qiviuq. The two yarns plied together create a unique hand-knitting fibre that has the weight of classic four-ply fingering and phenomenal yardage. A little luxury goes a long way.

For her Polar Seas yarn, Wendy created a range of vibrant colours like Dorset Blue, Huckleberry, Fireweed, and Arctic Autumn. They speak of the richness of the Arctic world and its uniquely precious natural resources. Every batch of yarn is hand-dyed to perfection by Wendy herself.

The knitter who touches qiviuq yarn only once is in danger of a lifelong addiction to its luxuriant softness. But the knitter who merely sees it once, with its brilliant jewel tones aglow in the light, is

in serious danger as well. The midnight sun, the icy blue ocean, carpets of wildflowers, and the changing seasons are all wrapped up in one supremely sensuous Canadian fibre.

Selling Canadian Knitting Yarns

Creating an attractive pattern book is the usual way to sell knitting yarns today, and the history of pattern publishing in Canada is a rich one. Studies show that most knitters choose a pattern before they choose the yarn to go with it. But it took some time for yarn manufacturers to realize this.

Charting A Path for Knitters: Pattern Books

The printed knitting pattern is very much a late Victorian invention. Its introduction and success depended on a level of literacy among women of all classes that was not achieved until public education was well advanced. Moreover, there was little point in publishing patterns until distribution channels were equally effective. The popular press blossomed in Victorian times and everything from novels — the famous "penny dreadfuls" — to knitting patterns could be readily bought for an affordable price.

Early Pattern Books

The very first printed patterns were included in books of general household management like *The Workwoman's Guide.* They recommended the use of generic types of wool that could be had on any farm, since few commercial yarns were available and few brand names were in general use at that time. The purpose of these early books was simply to teach the art of knitting, not to sell yarn.

The industry prophet who took printed patterns one step further and first made a connection between selling yarns and pattern books together was John Paton, Son, & Company. In the last years of the nineteenth century, the weight categories of yarns and the calibration of needles became standardized. This made it possible to recommend specific materials for specific projects and to assume success from following them.

Patons' first book, the *Knitting and Crochet Book,* was published in 1896. It was 228 pages long, included over one hundred patterns with items for every member of the family, and was priced at one shilling. The *Universal Knitting Book,* published three years later, was a slimmer volume of sixty-one pages and sold for just one penny. Its popularity was enormous, and it was republished many times.

The text was enriched by instructive maxims and literary quotations for the edification of the working knitter. One suitably exhortatory message read:

Costly thy habit as thy purse can buy, but not expressed in fancy; rich, not gaudy.

— *Shakespeare*

Another perhaps less well-received quotation was:

Nothing lovelier can be found in woman than to study household good.

— *Milton*

Moral pronouncements aside, the *Universal Knitting Book* was very advanced for its time. It had excellent engravings showing the shape and patterning of most garments, including precise renderings of the finest lace stitches. Such illustrations were a decided help when knitting new and complicated garments for the first time.

Printed patterns enlarged the knitter's traditional world by leaps and bounds.

Standardizing Pattern Notation: The Birth of K2, P2

The world has seen many improvements in pattern notation from the earliest written patterns to our own times.

Following an early nineteenth century pattern is apt to be rather confusing. In *The Workwoman's Guide,* for example, not only were there no abbreviations for common stitches but terms as familiar and essential to today's knitting as "purl" and "yarn over" were not in use. Pattern notation was clumsy and long winded, and the pattern writer was obliged to clearly define the exact motion of the fingers for every stitch. A pattern for "French Stitch" read:

Set on the stitches in fours, leaving two over.

Turn the first stitch,

Turn the thread back,

Knit two stitches together,

Bring the thread in front,

Knit a stitch, thus forming a new loop,

Bring the thread again in front,

Turn a stitch, one rib or pattern is then complete.

By the end of the nineteenth century, the term "purl" was well understood and abbreviations like k2 p2 began to appear in pattern books. "Slipping" stitches and "passing the slipped stitch over" had also become established vocabulary by that time.

Thus, the building blocks of knitting to a pattern, as we know it, were in place by the year 1900 and the stage set for wider horizons and an infinity of knitting possibilities. No longer would knitters be limited to the patterns of their own community or family. New garments could be created using new techniques and stitches. Many traditional knitting skills were undoubtedly lost when the printed pattern came into being and the world grew larger, but many new skills were learned and were passed on as far and as fast as the printed word could travel. The knitting life was immeasurably enriched.

Our own time has also sponsored change — some would call it complication — in the notation of printed patterns. Mary Maxim's "Graph Style" patterns became enormously popular in the 1950s and prepared knitters en masse for the convenience of working from diagrams rather than words. They introduced Canadians to the concept of a visual presentation of individual stitches, instead of a mere photograph of the finished garment.

In recent years, an increasing number of pattern books have contained schematic diagrams that picture the shape of each garment and specify the key measurements of every pattern piece. These not only help knitters knit to fit but also provide essential information for those who wish to recreate garments in yarns other than those specified. Schematics improve the ease of pattern selection because important features of garment construction are visible at a glance.

The most recent trend in notation is the use of symbolcraft in knitting patterns. Symbolcraft is a universal form of knitting notation using small marks. Each mark represents a different stitch or a different operation such as "k2tog." Symbolcraft patterns are written in graph form. Each mark is placed inside a square that represents one stitch. No words need appear on the graph itself, but a legend is usually published somewhere within the pattern book. It correlates symbols with familiar abbreviations. Even complex cables can be readily represented by these symbols.

The great advantage of symbolcraft is that it is virtually a wordless system, therefore, it does not need translation. Perhaps it harkens back to a centuries-old form of passing on knitting knowledge. Once it has been rendered in symbols, the same knitting pattern can then be sold in many different countries speaking many different languages.

Since most knitters readily memorize patterns and symbols, there may someday be little need for words at all. In one century, we have both built a language of knitting abbreviations and made it obsolete. We have also created a world of international knitters and of cross-cultural knitting ties and have established a huge market for printed patterns.

Selling knitting patterns has become an end in itself, not merely a means of selling yarn. Market conditions demand flexible patterns that can accommodate the large number of interchangeable yarns now available. In today's world where many consider hand knitting to be expendable and knitting skills are disappearing among the young, all

yarn sellers know that they have more to gain by encouraging knitting at large than they have to lose by tying patterns irrevocably to specific yarns.

Canada's yarn producers have had wonderful success in creating patterns that sell yarn. But like others in their place the world over, all the money they have spent creating today's lively knitting scene has never solved that one perennial purchase problem — persuading knitters to buy enough yarn at one time to complete their project.

Pattern Books in Canada

Before the company established a mill in Toronto in 1931, Patons yarns were sold in Canada through *Eaton's Catalogue*. Its pattern books came to Canada with its yarns and became the cornerstone of the great Beehive pattern empire that continues to be a powerful force in Canadian knitting today. If long-term brand loyalty to one publisher of pattern books exists in Canada, it is surely to patterns published by Patons & Baldwins. Continuing demand for classic books like *Beehive for Bairns,* nearly fifty years old and still appreciated, ensures that they are often republished.

By the 1920s, every yarn manufacturer had realized the importance of published patterns. Consumer confidence in the predictability of results grew, and they quickly became the source of knitting inspiration that they are today. Even the names of some early pattern books linger in our memories and remind us of the great number of Canadian yarn companies that have long since vanished, the casualties of business amalgamations and ever-increasing industry concentration.

For many years, Monarch knitting books were rivals in popularity to Beehive. A great many Monarch instruction books were published, beginning some time after 1910 when the Monarch Knitting Company of Dunnville, Ontario, was incorporated until the late 1960s when it closed. The very names of Monarch yarns lent an exciting cosmopolitan appeal to a homegrown product. Monarch Dove, Monarch Andalusian, and Monarch Crepe de Laine, in colours like Maybud, Maroon, Strawberry Ice, and Trublu strike responsive chords in our collective knitting memory.

Some of yesterday's pattern books were remarkable for their recognizable Canadian style. This expressed itself less in the shaping of garments, which usually conformed to classic lines, than in the pattern motifs themselves.

The maple leaf was the most familiar motif of all. On socks, sweaters, mittens, and hats, our national emblem made an attractive design that had lots of possibilities for interpretation. Knitters were on intimate terms with its contours long before it was confirmed as our national symbol in 1965 when the national flag was proclaimed. Maple leaves were used in coats of arms granted in 1868 to Ontario and Quebec and in the Canadian coat of arms granted in 1921. The maple leaf was also used on regimental badges in World War I and World War II. Dozens of fascinating knitting graphs were published for maple leaves in every stage of development. Some rather adventurous ones called for green yarn!

The magnificent caribou must surely have been a close second among Canadian motifs for knitters. It is the symbol of Canada's north and is still represented on our twenty-five cent piece. Older pattern books usually referred to it as "the reindeer." The caribou is still a special favourite in Newfoundland where the animals themselves are plentiful and easily observed. NONIA's most famous hand-knit sweater bears a caribou motif, and it has been consistently popular for nearly fifty years.

The undistinguished beaver even put in an occasional patriotic appearance in our knitting books, but our need to identify with this unprepossessing symbol of Canada seems to have been less strong. Once pursued for its elegant fur, Canada's largest rodent made a rather unimpressive and possibly unrecognizable subject when rendered in yarn.

Many garments were given Canadian names even though their patterns were not expressly symbolic. The "Miss Calgary" sweater, the "Temagami" vest, and the "Cape Breton Bush Jacket" kept a panoramic sense of our vast country always before us as our fingers worked. Canadian knitters have never experienced a national identity crisis.

Knitting and Lifestyle: The Challenge of Promotion

Patterns are undoubtedly a good way to advertise knitting yarns, but they were used to sell other things too. Lux pattern books, published annually in Canada between 1938 and 1958, except for several years during World War II, were created to sell soap.

Lux knitting patterns were beautiful and well written. They naturally devoted generous amounts of space to instructing conscientious knitters in the art of washing woollies. Their teaching was very detailed indeed, often taking up several pages. They used every promotional device including slogans, songs, and cartoons to depict the tremendous social penalties derived from wearing knits that were less than fresh.

The makers of Lux soap also sponsored a popular radio programme that was on the airwaves in 1942. The knitting pattern book for that year carried, complete with musical notation, the jingle that accompanied this programme. It was called Dolly's Daily Dipper Song.

Oh, I'm a Daily Dipper,
I treat my sweaters right.
I often give my sweaters
A dip in Lux at night.

If you're slow to wash your sweaters,
You take an awful chance,
For a girl who isn't dainty
Rates zero in romance.

Lux keeps a sweater dainty,
It keeps it fitting right.
It keeps the texture fluffy,
It keeps the color bright.

Join the Daily Dippers,
Who treat their sweaters right.
Does the sweater that you're wearing
Need a dip in Lux tonight?

When the manufacture of Lux Soap Flakes was discontinued in 1958, the knitting pattern books were too. What a loss to today's knitters!

In these glamorous times, the relationship between selling yarn and selling soap flakes is not as close as it once was. Peoples' lives have changed so greatly that to associate knitting with household drudgery, be it ever so necessary or amusing, would communicate the wrong message indeed.

Instead, knitting has grown wings and flown with that rallying cry of our own times, the environmental movement. It is a fortuitous pairing that brings the concerns of thoughtful people with a surging interest in fibre arts and in working with natural materials together with those working to preserve our planet.

Wool City International, a New Zealand-based company, has initiated some highly successful joint promotions between itself and various international branches of the World Wildlife Fund. It has designed marvellously coloured contemporary sweaters that feature motifs of endangered species of flowers and plants and butterflies and birds, using the symbols, patterns, and vibrant colours of the natural world. It also supplies affordable yarn kits of 100% Perendale wool, an extremely soft yarn that comes from a breed of sheep unique to New Zealand.

A successful joint promotion with the Canadian branch of the World Wildlife Fund took place in 1989. Their appealing promotional brochure linked the two messages of knitting and environmental concern in a way that was indeed persuasive. It advertised:

This pure natural New Zealand wool comes direct to you from the pollution free green and lovely pastures of that South Pacific "little Canada." Like Canadians, New Zealanders (and their sheep) share a common ideal of conservation and clean living. The naturalness of pure wool fibre is an expression of this ideal. Pure...and natural.

Response was enthusiastic. Wool City International realized that it had tapped a new market for hand knitting, one that is now firmly in place for the 1990s. It had reached Canadians who did not ordinarily think of knitting for themselves. Not only did Wool City International accept the opportunity of creating a beautiful garment, it took up the challenge of making the world a better place in which to live.

The relationship between lifestyle and knitting continues to be close, even though the lifestyles themselves may change. But today's ways of living are more threatening to our art. Travel and fitness are considered more desirable and glamorous than the satisfactions of a comfortable evening spent creating something lovely at home, and young people are not acquiring knitting skills as they once did. These are challenging times indeed.

The World Wildlife Foundation and Wool City International, a New Zealand-based company, link environmental awareness with hand knitting by jointly promoting attractive sweater designs such as this.

Women's Magazines

Nobody keeps in touch with changing Canadian lifestyles better than Canada's women's magazines. Happily, from the oldest to the newest, they have always been wonderful supporters of hand knitting and have done a great deal to draw the Canadian knitting scene together.

Chatelaine first appeared in March 1928, and in these early years, the masthead bore the charming subtitle "Mistress of her Castle." *Chatelaine* explained its early mission as "serving the chatelaine of Canada with authoritative information on housekeeping, child care, beauty and fashion and with entertaining fiction and articles of national interest."[59] It still does this successfully today.

Regular coverage of knitting began immediately. One early issue contained a pattern for "A Cosy Cape for Cool Days" nearly back-to-back with a timely article on "The New Woman of Russia." From the very beginning, *Chatelaine* was able to artfully combine articles on the minutiae of womens' daily concerns with an awareness of significant happenings in the world at large.

Its skillful editors were always able to evoke the many moods and motives of the knitter, from a mother's delight in knitting things for her children to the enjoyment of a few peaceful, private moments of knitting pleasure.

Ingenious practical tips on important topics like the care of woollens were carefully read by Canadian women who have always waged war on moths and rust. One article recommended the following treatment:

When the good old summertime comes, wrap them in plenty of newspapers. Moths don't read and newspapers don't appeal to them. They adore to snuggle into the cosy folds and lay their eggs, so don't spare the moth balls, and put them away clean. Moths feed on dirt.[60]

The *Chatelaine* of today continues to showcase the work of Canadian knitters and knitwear designers, commissioning and promoting new designs with an express Canadian theme. For more than sixty years, *Chatelaine* has led the knitting life along with us.

Canadian Living magazine appeared on the scene in 1975, long after *Chatelaine* had made its mark on knitters. It was a surprise to many Canadians who, in those years, had begun to fear the loss of some of our cultural footings. Launching a new periodical with a determined Canadian focus in a market where the competition was daunting

must have seemed hubristic indeed. From the very beginning, however, *Canadian Living* was a magazine that made us feel good about ourselves and proud of our achievements.

In the years since its launch, *Canadian Living* has featured nearly one hundred and fifty items of knitting interest, from patterns for knitting Hudson's Bay sweaters for cabbage patch dolls to the most elegant high fashion sweaters by famous Canadian hand-knitting designers.

Canadian Living has an exciting way of finding knitting stories and of bringing them to its readers. In 1982, when the Cowichan Indians of British Columbia made sweaters as official wedding presents for Prince Charles and Lady Diana Spencer, *Canadian Living* was there to interview the knitter and to provide a similar design for Canadian knitters. When television's Charlie Farquharson needed a new sweater in 1988, *Canadian Living* gave him one and covered it for us in a memorable article titled:

Canada's swetter boy gits hisself a noo nit: Charlie Farquharson's favrit cadygun iz so aynchunt it's in vague again.[61]

Everybody was happy to see him better dressed, but his spelling remained beyond help.

From the Fundy Fisherman Sweater to the Wheatsheaf Aran, from the Cottage Craft Sweater to the Newfoundland Trigger Finger Mitt, *Canadian Living* brings Canadian knitting to Canadians.

Crafts Plus magazine is the new kid on the block among magazines for knitters in Canada. Launched in 1985 with knitting as its central focus, it has been successful since its first promotional campaign. This immediate popularity is an indicator of the strong appetite that Canadians have for their own knitting news. We find it hard to get enough.

Canada's Yarn Retailers

In Canada, a great many balls of yarn are sold in department stores every year and Canadian manufacturers do a thriving business in private label yarn, but the neighbourhood yarn shop is often the link between individual knitters and all of the world's great knitting yarn treasures.

Canada's yarn retailers are a hardy breed of independent individuals. Selling yarn is surely one of the most labour-intensive forms of retailing in the business world. Making a single sale, necessitates matching ephemeral personal tastes in colour with preferences for certain fibres or

Nancy Vivian, owner of the Craft Cottage in Richmond, B.C., is one of Canada's most enthusiastic hand-knitting retailers. Her attractive shop is well known to knitters in the greater Vancouver area.

blends. These must work together with an appealing pattern that has just the right size and style details. Retailers must also have sufficient yarn in stock in the correct weight for the pattern.

Yarn retailers must have the skills of mathematicians to calculate yarn requirements, to adjust patterns, and to operate their businesses on a sound financial basis. They must have a simultaneous feel for the smart fashion sense of a society woman and the outlandish dress of a pop star, and know which of these role models any one of their customers seeks to emulate on any given day. They are among the world's best teachers who must effectively communicate the mechanics of a medieval art to people in a hurry. They must be social workers at heart, for knitters love to pour out their troubles over a few stitches in a friendly store. They must have the patience of Job to untangle their customers' mistakes without ruffling their feathers. And they must still figure out how to make a business with such a high level of service and a disproportionately low average sale figure pay its way.

On the positive side, yarn retailers work in a creative environment full of remarkable textures and colours. Their work is based on encouraging people, not policing or controlling them or involving themselves in some of the other distasteful aspects of the world of work. The satisfactions are abundant, for, above all else, selling yarn is a people-loving business. Yarn retailers know that they are a positive force in a difficult world.

Their business has its problems. There are now thousands of hand-knitting yarns made around the world from the least expensive synthetics to the rarest luxury fibres. Each is made in a great many shades that, like lipsticks, now come and go on a seasonal fashion cycle where once they were fixed points in a turning world.

The great number of options available to retailers is both an opportunity and a problem. The opportunity to stock beautiful and distinctive yarns has never been greater, but the problem of matching them with buyers quickly enough to pay the bills leaves a wide margin for error and there is not much security on which to fall back. Many retailers have paid the ultimate price for following their personal inclinations and stocking too many premium yarns in economy conscious neighbourhoods. Others have fallen victim to rising commercial rents and to changes in retailing that are beyond their control.

To compensate for some of the vulnerabilities of the yarn business, retailers have shown a talent for promotion second to none. Independent yarn shops usually have a high profile in their local business associations. They sponsor sports teams and take part in community events. They maintain firm connections with craft programmes for senior citizens, with the textile guilds and groups where professionals gather, and with the school and recreational programmes where young knitters begin their lifelong interest.

They write columns in local newspapers and organize fashion shows and weekend craft events. They have learned to maximize the use of their

The Getaway Gang, a group of enthusiastic Toronto area knitters and yarn retailers, has sponsored more than eighteen craft weekends. Members include (left to right) Joan Warren, Bev Thompson, Flo Johnson, and Alison Ahara.

Today's yarn retailers do more than just stick to their knitting. They also take an active part in community activities. Village Yarns of Islington, Ontario, has sponsored many ball teams, including some that were all male.

mailing lists and to create eye catching displays that attract new customers or start local knitting rages. Most yarn shops offer affordable courses to advance and encourage knitting skills, as well as dispensing countless unscheduled hours of free personal help. They seldom leave a struggling knitter out in the cold.

It is a full life, and one that is more often lived for sheer enjoyment than for profit, for many yarn retailers love knitting and love people more than they love money. Every one of them believes that making better knitters will make a better world.

Needles and Notions: Tools of the Trade

The manufacturing of knitting needles, indeed of pins and needles of any type, is a complex industrial process. Bishop Rutt, the English knitting historian, explains why knitting only became common in England in Elizabethan times:

Knitting needles could not easily be made. Steel rods required a high degree of skill from a whitesmith hammering away to produce them. Fine metal rods could be easily produced only after the art of drawing steel through perforated plates was perfected. This happened in England during the reign of Elizabeth I.[62]

The complexity of making needles was so well known that economist Adam Smith, writing in England in 1776, used it as an illustration of the principle of division of labour in his *Wealth of Nations*. Many first year economics students are familiar with his lengthy account which here is much abridged.

To take an example, therefore, from a very trifling manufacture,...the trade of the pinmaker; a workman not educated to this business (which the division of labour has rendered a distinct trade), nor acquainted with the use of the machinery employed in it ...could scarce, perhaps, with his utmost industry, make one pin in a day...But in the way in which this business is now carried on, ...one man draws out the wire, another straights it, a third cuts it, a fourth points it, a fifth grinds it at the top for receiving the head; to make the head requires three distinct op-

erations; to put it on is a peculiar business, to whiten the pins is another; it is even a trade by itself to put them into the paper...[63]

The reader begins to appreciate the feelings of the sorcerer's apprentice, but the message of complexity is loud and clear.

By the middle of the nineteenth century, a great variety of manufactured knitting needles were available in England. *The Workwoman's Guide* described the following tools of the trade:

Knitting pins or needles, as they are variously called, are made of iron or brass, for common use, and steel for best. They can be procured of every size and thickness, and are sold in sets, each set containing four pins. These sets cost from 1/8d. to 2d. each, according to the metal and size.

Special purpose needles of clever design and elegant materials are not, it seems, inventions of our own time, for the account continued:

Ivory, bone, whalebone, steel, rosewood, ebony and cane pins, of a larger size and thickness are employed for knitting coverlids [sic], boots, carpets, and other thickly knit articles. These are sometimes twenty inches or two feet long, and have a knob at one end to prevent the stitches from slipping off. Of these pins two or three form the set.[64]

Factory-made needles with standardized calibrations were in short supply in Canada in the early years, but this did not impede the determined and resourceful knitters of days gone by. The Cowichan Indians, for example, were known to have used whale bone, deer bone, telephone wire, and bamboo chopsticks to knit with.

Many Canadian knitters learned their art on needles made by a father, husband, or brother from the materials at hand. One Newfoundland woman remembered:

Daddy used to make wire knitting needles for us sometimes. Around barrels, sometimes, you'd get some small wires. Daddy would cut them off and sharpen them to points on a grind stone. They'd come off right smooth and nice.[65]

Other Newfoundlanders had equally imaginative ideas. In one community, needles were made from the metal spokes found in an umbrella. In another area, the local men made wooden knitting needles that were called "skivvers." This descrip-

Early twentieth century knitting needles and notions sold in Canada by the T. Eaton Company.

tive term was clearly appropriate. The *Newfound-land Dictionary* reports that the original meaning of this word was "a skewer, especially a forked stick on which fish are impaled or strung through the gills in carrying." It could also be used to describe a very thin person!

The manufactured knitting needles that were eventually used in Canada came from Britain and bore the British numbering system. Bishop Rutt shed some light on the knitting needle industry and on the trade-names that we recognize today. He wrote that by the 1920s a series of amalgamations had reduced the number of manufacturers in Britain to three: William Hall, Henry Milward, and Abel Morrall. Hall and Milward amalgamated in 1930, continuing to make needles under the name of Milward. In 1973, this firm became part of the Patons group, and in 1983, Abel Morrall, whose needles were sold under the Aero trademark, also joined the group. Bishop Rutt also reported that the German company Rump, which uses the trade-name Inox, is the largest producer of knitting needles in the world.

In the early 1980s, bamboo needles from Japan became available and were very popular because of their light weight, particularly with arthritic knitters.

Bishop Rutt stated that British needles were made to the British Standard Steel Wire Gauge so the early makers of home-made wire needles were on the right track. The bell gauge helped knitters to determine the size of the needles they owned.

The arrival of the metric system caused some difficulty for knitters who could envision a number 11 needle, for example, but had no concept of the dimensions of a millimetre. Explaining the re-numbering process Bishop Rutt wrote:

When metrication came in 1975, British sizes were given the nearest approximate metric designation (not always accurate to the sec-ond decimal place) but vulgar fractions such as 3 3/4 were adopted. This oddity is partly due to the distinction between the standard scale of [European] sizes, which goes in half millimetre steps, and the British scale, which keeps the quarter and three-quarter millimetre steps between 2 and 4 millimetres. Needles of 2 1/2 mm and 3 1/2 mm are not used in Brit-ain.[66]

Canada naturally followed the British model, but things in this country became complicated by the influence of the entirely original numbering system used in the United States, which is like the pre-metric British system but with sizes numbered in the reverse order. Thus, a number 10 needle in the United States is very large; whereas in Canada it is very small. All in all, metric numbering became safest for every knitting nation.

Canadian knitters have never permitted themselves to become spoiled by an abundance of knitting notions. In fact, we have spurned most "knitters' helpers" in favour of mastering good, traditional techniques. We are a pragmatic people. As late as the 1940s, instructions for knitting cables in Canadian pattern books were given without the use of a cable needle. This tricky technique called for dropping the stitches to be twisted, knitting the intervening stitches, then backing up to pick up the dropped stitches, still presumably hanging intact. The simple invention of the cable needle, it seems, had much to offer the world and even Canadians embraced it.

The great masters of inventing clever knitting notions are, of course, the Americans. Over the years, the back pages of their craft publications have advertised a fascinating array of ingenious devices to improve life for the knitter. The great majority of these were designed to solve that continuous problem — tangle-free argyle and Fair Isle knitting. The goal remains elusive.

CHAPTER 5

Who Knits In Canada ?

What do a Canadian labour leader and a Canadian hockey player have in common? What do a washroom attendant and a Father of Confederation have in common? Knitting is a common thread that joins the lives of the great and the less great in Canada; a country in which men and women, young and old, knit.

The strongest images of knitting known to most Canadians are found in our shrines to family memory. Knitting and the symbol of the hearth are inextricably blended in the Canadian consciousness — mothers knitting at kitchen tables while children study their lessons, grandmothers knitting beside the bedsides of the sick, and sisters knitting for their husbands-to-be.

William Gough provides us with a tender word portrait of artist David Blackwood's maternal grandmother in her Newfoundland home. It is suffused with the warm, mystical glow of childhood memory, a glow that intensifies as we grow older.

My great grandmother with her yarn swift and her knitting. About 1930.

The lamplight would pour warm along her face and spill over knitting fingers, and David would watch and listen. At night he'd creep out of bed and watch the moon pull caplin spawn through the waters — this was Bragg's Island, forever.[67]

The magic of soft, quiet moments of loving intimacy and the surging spirit of place melt together, making an indelible imprint on the developing memory of a sensitive child.

Notables Who Knit

The foyers of Canadian public life are filled with knitting personages whose support of this private field of endeavour is largely unrecognized.

Indeed, the highest in the land have often taken up their needles to make a uniquely personal statement in yarn. Let us now give credit where credit is due.

It was a great surprise to Canadians when the New Brunswick Museum recently discovered knitting patterns among the papers of a Father of Confederation. The patterns were found in the records of Sir Leonard Tilley (1818–1896). There were three patterns in all, one for a knitted blanket, one for a "knitted knee cap," and one for a "rainbow scarf."

The patterns were all handwritten, each in a different hand, and the writing has not yet been positively identified. Was the great man himself a closet knitter? This seems rather unlikely. It is more probable that his wife, Lady Tilley, collected patterns jotted down on odd bits of paper, just as confirmed knitters do today. One thing is certain — knee caps got cold in the great houses of the nation as well as in the small.

The knitting pattern for a "Rainbow Scarf" was one of three patterns found among the papers of Sir Leonard Tilley, a Father of Confederation.

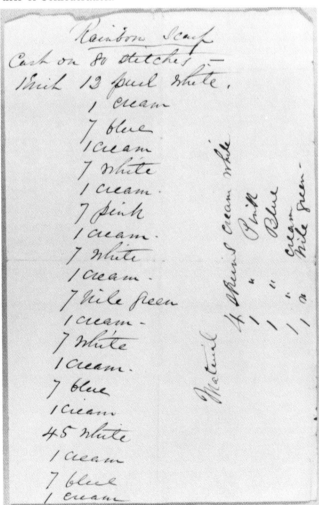

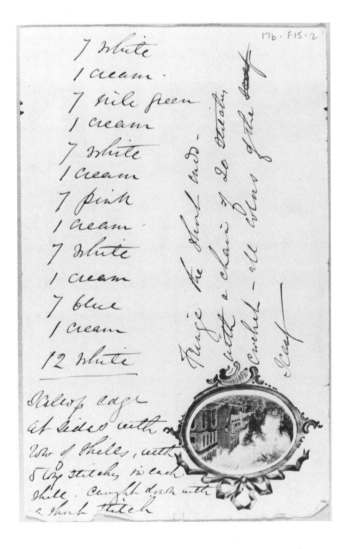

Jacques Plante (1929–1986), long-time goaltender for the Montreal Canadiens hockey team, was renowned as a knitter. Some of his acquaintances say that he even knit his own long underwear. He claimed that the rhythmic activity settled his pre-Stanley Cup nerves.

Labour leader Grace Hartman, an excellent and well-known knitter, has often been photographed wearing sweaters of her own making. Although she looks comfortable and grandmotherly, most people remember her as the first woman to hold the top position in a Canadian union and remember too that, in 1981, Grace was jailed for counselling an illegal strike. Guts and knitting go together.

Members of the Canadian Opera Company are known to be avid knitters. They always have something stimulating to work on during the long and ponderous waits for airplanes when on tour. Musicians in some of Canada's top orchestras knit for the same reason. One such knitter was most embarassed when she dropped her needle during a particularly quiet passage in a very important overture. Happily, they were only in rehearsal.

Ballerina Veronica Tennant knits, thereby giving her legs a rest from time to time. The list of notable knitters goes on and on.

Everyday Knitters

Canada's knitting notables are many, but at the other end of the social spectrum is the everyday knitter. In comparison to other countries, Canada's knitting culture rests safely in agile, capable hands and is in little danger of disappearing. Statistics indicate that seventy percent of Canadian women aged sixteen and over know how to knit, although only half of these are active in any given year.

There is no such thing as a proper time and place for knitting. Everyday knitters will pick up their needles anywhere for a few snatched moments of enjoyment, whether it be a lunch hour spurt of creativity or an agreeable way of passing time in transit.

Knitting on the Toronto Transit Commission is a popular way to lessen the tedium of big city transportation.

Some everyday knitters are easy to spot. Washroom attendants at Toronto's Maple Leaf Gardens, for example, are particularly enthusiastic in their pursuit of knitting. The cafeterias and lunchrooms of our nation echo with the click of needles, particularly in the hectic weeks that precede Christmas each year. It seems that many Canadians would rather be knitting.

Men Who Knit

Most Canadian men will tell you that they learned to knit as boys, but that they did not progress beyond the pot holder level of competence.

It was none other than Lord Baden-Powell of Gilwell who encouraged Canadian boys to learn to knit, and every Wolf Cub took his exhortations very seriously. Lord Baden-Powell argued his case in *The Wolf Cub's Handbook.* That august compendium of useful lore that was first published in England in December 1916 under the title *Scouting for Boys* and was dedicated "to Rudyard Kipling, who has done so much to put the right spirit into our rising manhood." A special Canadian edition was published in 1954 because Lord Baden-Powell realized that it should be "altered and amended to suit Canadian Scouts in their own land."

His advice on knitting comes in the chapter titled "Thirteenth Bite" and is lumped together with such other moral imperatives as "savings," "collections," and "God Save the Queen." Baden-Powell wrote:

> One of the things that a Cub ought to be able to do is to knit. This is not at all difficult to learn, and it comes in very useful when making things for yourself or for other people.
> It is particularly useful if you go out into the wilds later on as a pioneer or explorer.
> Shackleton's men in the Arctic expeditions were all able to knit their own socks and mitts, and I have known many hunters and travellers and soldiers, especially those from Scotland, who could always knit their own stockings.

Thus making socks should not be considered less manly than wearing them. What was good for Arctic explorers was good enough for Canadian boys. But as time went by, employment in the pioneering and exploring lines became seriously limited, and most boys forgot their need for knitting skills. Knitting among women became the general rule in Canada while men neglected it, perhaps conforming to the safe principle of "one knitter per family."

But when today's men are encouraged to take up their needles, they often pursue knitting with the singlemindedness of the true devotee and the professionalism of their work shows it.

The following stories of three men who knit typify the possibilities of life for the knitting male.

Russell O'Brien: Knitting With A Twist

Collisions between the art world and the knitting world always cause interesting sparks to fly, and big sparks do indeed fly when Russell O'Brien picks up his needles. Russell's background is the world of fashion illustration and theatre design, but today he makes much of his living by knitting.

Knitter Russell O'Brien is not tied down to conventional ideas of what knitting should be.

But this is knitting with a difference. It would perhaps be better to think of Russell's creations as works of the imagination executed in stitches. Think, for example, of his plan to knit a tea set for his 1991 exhibition in Haliburton, Ontario. And while Russell does knit garments, there are not many neat little pullovers or buttoned cardigans among them. His unusually vast and extravagant garment shapes are decorated with verve and humour. His Group of Seven sweater, for example, bore seven little painters, all knit in infinitely tiny three-dimensional stitches. It is Russell's exuberance and energy and his break with traditional themes that will take younger Canadian knitters into the 1990s with flair.

Don Colvin: Knitter to the Stars

Don Colvin, Canada's very own Knitter to the Stars, is a highly accomplished knitter who once operated his own yarn shop and sometimes teaches knitting at the Haliburton School of Fine Arts.

Don knits for the rich and famous. He has designed and made sweaters for Bette Midler, Burt Reynolds, Loretta Young, and John Boorman, among others. Sometimes he is asked to knit for the stage or screen and sometimes for a star's personal wardrobe. Appreciative actors have ordered copies of sweaters that they wore on screen for themselves or have requested custom designs for their friends.

Don knits what his clients want and can tailor his garments to a perfect fit despite the whimsical instructions that world-famous non-knitters are often apt to give. He also meets knitting deadlines that would strike fear into the hearts of less professional knitters. Movie stars, it must be acknowledged, are not the most patient of people nor are they known for understanding the constraints and subtleties of the knitter's art.

Don learned to knit from his father, a man who often helped his son out with a tight deadline or a large contract. His work apart, as a second-

Don Colvin designed and knit this sweater, commissioned by actress Bette Midler as a gift for a friend.

generation male knitter, Don really is something quite special.

Mark Radigan

Not every male knitter feels the need to hit the society high spots with his skill. Mark Radigan, a young man who was born with Spina Bifida and is paralyzed below the waist, makes room for his knitting among the demands of a full-time job and a busy life. Like most Canadians, Mark's mother taught him to knit. His first project, at the age of six, was a sweater for his favourite teddy bear. These days, it is more likely that his wife, his family, or his friends are the lucky beneficiaries of his skill. Mark has also done contract work for knitwear designers and custom knitting. Mark Radigan's sweaters are colourful, comfortable extravaganzas of skillful knitting that comes from the heart.

Canada's male knitters are no longer the pioneers and explorers of the untamed wilderness — they have become pioneers and explorers of style and craftsmanship.

Little Knitters

Most active hand knitters in Canada today learned the art as children. In fact, there is a direct correlation between the age of learning and the active pursuit of knitting later: the younger the learner, the more lively the interest.

Knitting Readiness

Most adults who learned to knit as children will tell you that they acquired the skill at about seven years of age, even though they may have played with yarn and needles prior to that. Children are

Mark Radigan's friends and family are often the lucky recipients of his stunning creations.

Nineteenth century knitters got an early start on learning
their art. Photograph circa 1870.

certainly capable of learning to knit at an even more tender age, and in places like the Shetland Islands where knitting was a common form of employment, girls often knit steadily from the age of four onwards and their behaviour was not considered precocious. By knitting the plain parts of garments, which their mothers later completed in pattern, they contributed to the family economy.

In our gentler world, seven years of age may also be a time of supreme knitting readiness, when intellectual and motor development are such that mastery is possible without undue frustration.

Learning to Knit

Most Canadians were taught to knit by a family member, usually a mother or a grandmother who had a bit of extra time and patience to spare. Grandmothers were indispensable members of the extended family. As one Newfoundland woman stated, "Old women always did mending, knitting, and making quilts. It took a lot of work off the young wife."

Grandmothers could be exacting task mistresses as well. My mother learned to knit as a young child. Her grandmother, whose home they shared, had been born in Scotland and was a staunch Presbyterian Sabbath-keeper. The little knitter was eager to practice her newly acquired skill, despite the prohibition against knitting on Sunday. When she was found closeted behind the dining room door with her knitting in her hand, she was told that she would have to remove every stitch with her teeth in heaven! Young knitters today seldom have this additional worry on their minds.

Occasionally, when there was no teacher in the home, some knitters taught themselves. These determined people had a natural talent for acquiring manual skills. Hilda Chaulk Murray quotes one woman's verbatim account of learning woolcraft by observation.

I'll tell 'e how I got that now, maid. In the evenings when I'd go around ... and see 'em then cardin' wool. I was only small and I'd see what they'd do. And when I'd see 'em cardin' I'd say: "Why can't I do that?" And I'd take up the cards when they'd put 'em down and try 'em and I learnt cardin'. And I'd see 'em with the spinnin' wheel. I used to always go to Aunt Polly's and Polly'd go out in the stable somewhere and I used to say: "I wonder can I run her wheel?" And I'd give it a try. So nice, and I said "I can spin." ... I was all there for

that. Go in anyone's house and see them sewing on the machine. I could knit sweaters, and stockin's and mitts, gloves, do anything. My mother never showed me cause Mother never knowed how to knit. I learned meself now, like that...[68]

For would-be knitters with no access to personal example, or for knitters who wanted to improve their techniques without bothering anyone, there were one or two books on the market that helped. Patons & Baldwins' *Woolcraft* was a popular booklet that was frequently reprinted. It contained complete directions in both words and pictures for forming the essential stitches and for conducting all basic knitting operations.

To most Canadians, Beehive's *Steps to Knitting* is by far the more familiar book. For many years, it was distributed to home economics classes throughout the country, and in its pages many of today's knitters can recognize the patterns they used for their first pair of bedroom slippers (ribbed, with a drawstring) or their first garter stitch tea cosy.

Brownies and Girl Guides

Although Wolf Cubs have given up their yarn and needles, Brownies and Girl Guides continue to be among the staunchest supporters of hand knitting in Canada. During World War II, they made a remarkable contribution to the war effort. In later years, they were active in knitting for Vietnamese civilians during the Vietnam War. Today, they continue to knit selflessly for many charitable causes. The many knitted toys that they make for hospitalized children are always sources of pleasure and expressions of understanding between young people.

Brownies must demonstrate a knowledge of knitting to achieve their Golden Hand, although alternative crafts are accommodated as well. According to the *Golden Hand Record* book that every Brownie keeps, the requirement is to:

Knit, crochet, weave or macrame one of the following: pot holder, afghan square or other simple article. Show how to begin and end it correctly.

More advanced knitters can earn the special "Knitter" badge by doing the following:

Knit or crochet two different articles, such as doll's clothes, household articles, or clothing.

Show the Tester how to begin and end an article of knitting or crocheting correctly. Show how to increase and decrease and how to do one fancy stitch.

Girl Guides qualify for their "Knitter" badge when they can demonstrate their ability to:

- Cast on and cast off.

- Increase and decrease.

- Follow printed instructions.

- Knit or crochet two of the following: doll blanket, doll garment, toy, hand or finger puppet, mitts, slippers or similar article.

- Make a display of various types and weights of yarn and show what each might be used for, or

- Visit a fair, museum or handicraft display and find out what types of articles have been knitted.

In a day when mothers and grandmothers are not always able to pass on their skills, we have much to thank the Brownie's and Girl Guides for.

WOOLY WORD SEARCH

```
S P I N D L E P C L E A N I M K P S
T A L T Y C C L U E A R O G N A H O
I S O B E S O Y A R N A H I G E V F
T I V E G U A G R R L N T F A S W T
C K L Y W O O L M A R K H R J E A C
H F A I R I S L E C A N R L I L S I
R B N D E L E B A L C O E P N D H L
E L O R R O L O C W D T A E U E I Y
B O L F S P I N S T E R D E P E N R
I O I A E S N R E T T A P H S N G C
F W N K D R E P R O C E S S E D N A
```

4-H Clubs across Canada have developed interesting materials to teach knitting to young people. This puzzle contains a total of thirty-four words relating to wool or knitting.

4-H Clubs

For decades, 4-H clubs have been among the most encouraging supporters of knitting in Canada. Nearly every province has developed impressive, high quality instructional materials aimed at preparing young hand knitters for a lifetime of satisfaction and creative achievement.

4-H clubs teach every level of knitting, from casting on and doing basic stitches to sophisticated design projects. Some clubs also offer programmes in wool preparation, hand spinning, and natural dyeing and they teach everything in a way that makes it fun. 4-H knitters learn all about the wider world of knitting fibres, their composition, and specific properties. They are taught excellent presentation skills, and they learn how to judge and evaluate knitted projects. Achievement is carefully monitored and given the recognition it deserves. In short, as they express it themselves, they "learn to do by doing." Theirs is perhaps the most comprehensive programme of instruction available to young Canadian knitters today.

Young Knitters and Their Heritage

Some cultural institutions have taken the praiseworthy step of connecting young knitters with the history of their craft and country. Montgomery's Inn is a delightful historic building that operates as a museum in the Toronto suburb of Etobicoke.

During school holidays one year, instructors at the inn decided to offer a basic programme for children to learn to knit. The beginning project was a typical nineteenth century object — a six-inch square hot pad — knit of cotton string — a simple and easy to work with material. The course lasted four days and emphasized the enjoyable mastery of technique, combined with a learn-at-your-own-pace atmosphere and plenty of time for practise.

On the first day, children were given needles with the stitches already cast-on and were taught the knit stitch. Purling came on Day Two. Casting-on followed on the third day, and the final day was reserved for consolidating and practising their new skills. Along with instruction, the workshop included a chance to experience the atmosphere of the inn by working in a different room each day and by serving traditional Canadian refreshments. To keep interest alive and to provide a break for struggling fingers, the programme also included a look at nineteenth century knitting tools, wool carding, spinning, dyeing, and other wool-related activities.

The programme at Montgomery's Inn was judged a success. It not only provided valuable

Montgomery's Inn, a charming nineteenth century building, was the site of a programme that introduced children to their Canadian knitting heritage.

skills but also placed the art of knitting into its social and cultural context for young Canadians. And perhaps it also created a lifelong knitter or two.

The Many Moods of Current Canadian Knitting

There are dozens, perhaps hundreds of Canadians who make their living from hand knitting. Canada does not have long-established commercial hand-knitting businesses as they do in Britain, for example, but we do have a warm appreciation of exquisite hand-made clothes and an appetite for more and more of them.

Canadians wear their hand knits with pride, with comfort, and with pleasure. Many of us live our lives at the centre of a mechanical and technological maelstrom that can threaten our sense of belonging and oneness with the world. While knitting itself is a pleasure, the simple act of donning a hand-knit sweater, with all the personalized attention and careful craftsmanship that it symbolizes, can revitalize the most world weary. People who wear hand knits just simply feel cared for.

A look at the work of some professional hand-knitting enthusiasts offers the merest hint of the verve and vivacity of Canadian hand-knitting designers. Knitting is not the easiest way to make one's fortune, and the sheer determination of these creative entrepreneurs contributed to their growing success.

The Fashion Knitters

The hand knits of some Canadian designers are a true feast for the senses. Sharon Oakley of Harmony Classics in Halifax makes her luxurious sweaters of the finest silks, supple ribbons, angoras, and laces. Her work is best known for its textures, from pearl encrusted collars to her unusual lace panel sleeves. To touch them is to bring a reminder of richness and elegance to the fingertips. She chose the name "Harmony Classics" because her designs are in tune with the times, combining the old with the new, the traditional craft of knitting with today's lifestyles and fashion-conscious looks.

Sharon's sweaters are frequent prize winners on the fashion scene and have received international recognition. Among other encouragements, she was commissioned to design unique sweaters for the masters of ceremonies at the 1987 Canada Games' opening ceremonies. With the help of fifty home knitters, she now produces more than three thousand sweaters per year and sells them throughout Canada and the United States.

Linda Laing of Montreal creates distinctive knits for women of distinction. She had already established her knitting business and was selling to shops in Canada and the United States when Mila Mulroney became one of her most enthusiastic clients. Now the two meet several times a year so that Mila can view the latest Linda Laing creations and choose the ones she wants. Mila has also given beautiful sweaters to several First Ladies and Heads of State. Foreign dignitaries who might have overlooked our flowering talents are now certain to know the worth of Canadian hand knitting.

Linda's sweaters are sold in exclusive boutiques in Montreal and New York. Her lush florals and exotic imagery communicate a personal vision of the rich natural world under her very own label of wearable art.

Smooth, sporty West Coast style is the trademark of Vancouver's Knitwear Architects, a fortuitous partnership between radio broadcaster and textile historian Margaret Meikle and interior designer Janice Tsuruda. Their sweaters have a clean and simple look that is ideal for the outdoor

Sharon Oakley, owner of Harmony Classics, designs elegant sweaters in her Halifax studio.

Linda Laing wearing her "Long Coat with Hollyhocks and Butterflies."

life for which British Columbia is famous. They also feature bold and distinctive style details like deep necklines, thick cables, and generous ribbed lapels.

Janice learned to knit as an adult and found fussy traditional designs and detailed patterns unnecessarily complicated. She simplified her shapes and textures so that they have a true "architectural" quality, each piece being a simple building block producing a beautiful finished product.

Meikle and Tsuruda have carried the architectural metaphor further and have designed a new form of knitting pattern for their garments. Designed with the principle of the construction blueprint in mind, it helps knitters to visualize their work as they proceed. Even first time knitters are delighted with the results.

Knitwear Architects has a handsome retail outlet for its designs, which it makes available as finished garments or in kit form. It also sells its own brand of natural fibre yarns and some unusual and exciting knitting accessories.

Toronto's Knitknetwork is one of the hottest hand-knitting businesses in that city's very warm fashion scene. The Knitknetwork is a partnership that resulted from many discussions between four determined and dyed-in-the-wool knitters and designers — Rachel MacHenry, Mags Kandis, Carey Nicholson, and Juju Harvey.

They are talented, they have energy, and their fashion hand knits are a breath of fresh air. Consider, for example, MacHenry's recent hat collection that included spiral specialties like the "Onion Dome" and the "Spotted Mini-curl," or the multiple wonders of her "Unicorn," "Bi-corn," and "Tri-corn" hats.

Members of the Knitknetwork collaborate on collections and designs and make their mark as individual designers as well. Their hard work and unique talents are beginning to gain them some well-deserved recognition. MacHenry, for example, is the first ever "knitter-in-residence" at the prestigious Harbourfront Craft Studio, and Harvey has had designs accepted by major fashion magazines. Kandis and Nicholson's knits are well known in Toronto fashion circles, and they continue to receive media attention. Knitknetwork's designs are sold in some Toronto boutiques.

Last summer the group was selected for Toronto's innovative Fashion Incubator program. The city-supported Incubator is a studio centre in the garment district that helps promising new designers launch their careers. It rents them space for a limited period, provides office support, and offers advice on design and business matters.

Pictured here on Vancouver's popular Kitsilano Beach, Knit-wear Architects' sweaters are ideal for the west coast open-air life.

The Knitknetwork at work in its studio in the middle of Toronto's fashion district. Pictured from left to right are Mags Kandis, Carey Nicholson, and Rachel MacHenry.

Rachel MacHenry wearing some of her unusual hats.

Knitknetwork has also taken part in international fashion shows in Europe where its designs were enthusiastically received.

Members of the Knitknetwork combine excellent practical skills and an intimate knowledge of their craft with a fresh vision of the possibilities of knitting. We look forward to its future.

The Folk Art Knitters

Canadian hand knits are not only fashionable and original but are also powerful mood alterers. Lynn Maclachlan's splendid folk art sweaters can vividly recall a summer meadow on even the coldest winter day. Bold slashes of colour lift the spirit and convey the designer's *joie de vivre*. Consider, for example, the restorative power of "white ducks on a paddy green background, with white barns and hearts on bands of navy," or the sheer visual witticism of two spotted black and white cows each facing one single slice of juicy pink watermelon.

Maclachlan sells her sweaters by mail order and at craft shows. She makes her designs available as kits so you too can wear a vigorous piece of Canadian art just for the knitting.

The bold Fair Isles from Cumberland County Knitters of Wallace, Nova Scotia, speak directly to

Lynn Maclachlan (left) surrounded by her distinctive Hand-made By Me sweaters at a craft show. Pictured here with her mother (right) who often lends a hand.

Lynn Maclachlan's charming designs have the freshness of folk art. Knitting one is as restorative as taking a country holiday.

the Canadian spirit about the exhilaration of the ski slope and the freedom of the skating rink. The company is owned by Richard Ratcliffe, a former navy man who once tried to retire. Its sweaters are a symbol of Nova Scotia outdoor style that has become familiar across Canada. Cumberland County sweaters have received a lot of publicity and were selected for wear by the officials of the 1990 World Figure Skating Championships and Ottawa's Winterlude celebrations.

Richard's wife Pat is also his designer, and her vibrant colour sense dominates Cumberland County's sweaters. Its "Live Lobster" sweater is a rich deep brown with white, forest green, and yellow Fair Isle accents. "Fundy Fog" is a soft, greyed lavender with a Fair Isle yoke in plum, lilac, and rose. Its geometric motifs combine the best of Old World knitting with a sharp, clear, distinctively Canadian look. Cumberland County markets finished sweaters through mail order, retail outlets, and craft shows.

Grand Manan Island's Whale Cove Knitters created these
beautiful sweaters in their seaside homes.

Cumberland County Knitters make beautiful sweaters that are at home in the Canadian climate.

Nancy Thomas and her knitters from Ontario's Niagara Peninsula also have a way with Canadian wildlife. Loons, ducks, flocks of sheep, and gaggles of geese all grace her attractive sweaters. Her colourful equestrian pullover evokes the thrill and motion of the hunt as vividly as an old-time hunting print. Country picture knits just do not come much better than these. Nancy sells her sweaters to retail outlets across Canada and in the United States.

Pulling on your whale-watching sweater made by the Whale Cove Knitters of New Brunswick's Grand Manan Island can make you feel the salt spray of the Bay of Fundy on your face, hear the cry of the gulls, or sense the peacefulness of a lupin-filled meadow.

In the same way as music, painting, and other art forms, Canadian hand-knit sweaters have the power to evoke memory and to stimulate desire.

Why Canadians Knit

Competitive and Commemorative Knitting

Canadian knitters are generous people who give endlessly of their time to make things for other people to wear. Their satisfaction usually comes from a job well done and from the expressions of appreciation that they receive. But many knitters who know the value of their work and the quality of their craftsmanship seek the recognition of a wider audience. They want to test their skills in a rigorous competitive environment.

Fairs and Exhibitions

The agricultural exhibitions and fairs held across our country have always been excellent *champs de bataille* for knitters seeking glory.

Canada has a long experience with such fairs. History records that the first agricultural exhibition in North America was held in Nova Scotia in 1765. Perhaps knitting was not part of the drawing card for this first fair, but by the nineteenth century home arts and crafts were well established on the exhibition circuit. Many knitters sought prizes year after year and planned their knitting projects with competition in mind.

Prairie Agricultural Fairs

Textile historian Marijke Kerkhoven made a detailed study of the prize-winner lists of agricultural fairs held in Alberta and Saskatchewan between 1879 and 1915. She found that knitting was the second most popular competitive textile craft, exceeded only by embroidery and that, as the years passed, the types of knitting entered in these contests changed.

In the early years, competitions were held for the best hand-knit underwear at the fairs Kerkhoven studied. Prizes were also awarded for many different types of socks and mittens. Prize categories were sometimes varied by type of yarn, with homespun yarns being a separate division until well into the twentieth century.

Kerkhoven's work also confirmed something that yarn producers have always known — that there are periodic rages for knitting, which ebb and flow according to mysterious forces. One of these rages peaked in the 1880s. Another crested in the years following 1909 when there was a marked increase in knitting interest. During this period, the number and variety of prize classes for knitting at agricultural fairs grew. The items that were entered in these later contests became more and more decorative, although competitions for the best socks and mittens always remained popular.

After 1900, prizes were awarded for finely-worked silk and cotton stockings. Mittens were divided into plain and fancy categories, the latter being sometimes made of silk. Knitting for the home became popular and counterpanes, doileys, and tablemats, as well as a whole range of baby clothes, became new categories of competition, mirroring changes in the quality of life in the prairie provinces. Kerkhoven found that Regina was a veritable hotbed of knitting, followed in order by Edmonton, Calgary, and Saskatoon. Knitters from Edmonton and Prince Albert in particular excelled at using homespun yarns.

As the years went by, knitters consumed by the pursuit of excellence in their work went further afield. The Canadian National Exhibition, held every summer in Toronto, became one of the greatest knitting competitions of them all.

The Canadian National Exhibition

No one knows the precise year in which the Canadian National Exhibition began holding competi-

An early display of Mary Maxim products at the Canadian National Exhibition.

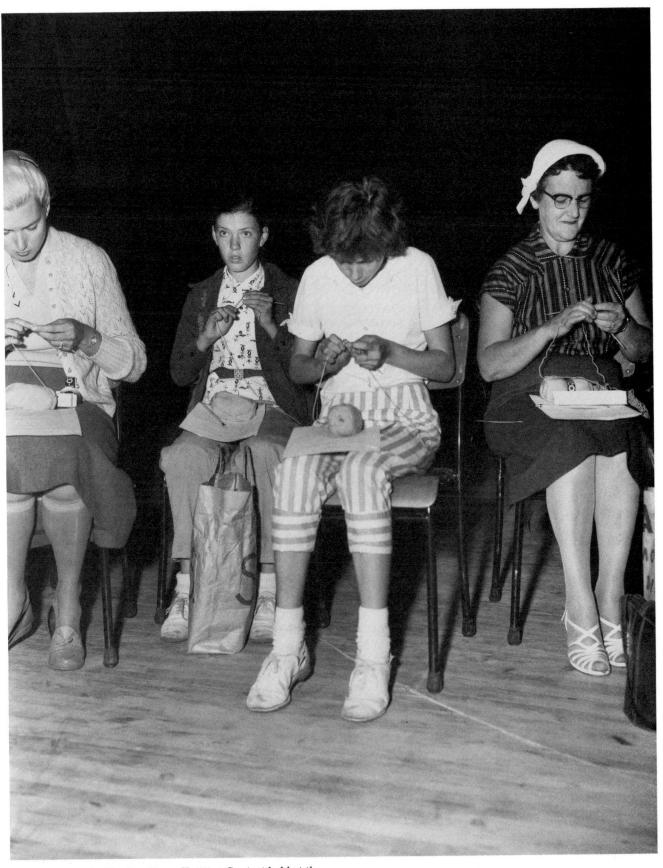

Participants in the Harding Yarns Knitting Contest held at the
Canadian National Exhibition concentrate on their work.

tions for crafts, but the Official Programme of 1899 clearly indicates an established interest. Saturday, September 2, 1899, was designated "Ladies' and Society Day" and the programme was arranged "under the special auspices of the Woman's Art Association and various women's societies of the City of Toronto." It included "a grand exhibit of women's work in the top gallery of the Main Building." In later years, the CNE established a Women's Committee (usually chaired by a man) to organize craft and needlework displays for enthusiastic competitors.

Knitting at the Canadian National Exhibition truly began to flourish under Kate Aitken, or "The Incredible Mrs. A.," as she became known. Her name became a household word to Canadians and under her energetic direction, interest in needlework thrived. Kate Aitken's career at the CNE began in 1923 and continued until 1952 when she was succeeded by the equally able Elsa Jenkins.

Prize lists from past years tell us much about the encouragement of Canadian knitters. Adults, children, the handicapped, and the elderly were all urged to compete. Contests were open to individual knitters, to groups of people, and to school classes. The categories for child knitters were divided still by age group so that there would be no unfair advantage. And like the great Olympian athletic contests of ancient Greece, knitting competitions at the CNE were entered more for glory than for pecuniary reward.

Prizes rarely exceeded $10.00 until recently.

Yarn companies found the CNE an excellent place to meet their customers face to face, to promote themselves, and to introduce new products. They advertised their yarns in the prize lists that were sent across Canada. Their product displays grew more and more inventive and imaginative. In most years, a special prize was given for knitting with pure wool. This prize was usually awarded by the Mary Maxim company, but occasionally the Wool Bureau or a different yarn company took a turn. The prize money ranged between twenty-five and fifty dollars, a real bonus considering the usual amounts of the awards.

Sometimes a special event or two would focus particular attention on knitting. In 1957, for example, Harding Yarns sponsored a knitting contest, held every afternoon at 5:00 p.m. in the Queen Elizabeth Building. Willing contestants were provided with an un-illustrated pattern for an unknown item, some needles, and a ball of Harding yarn. When the signal to begin was given, they fell to the project at hand, each woman assuming the position of a true competitive knitter. After an appropriate period, time was called, the results compared, and a winner chosen. The prize was a lovely wristwatch. Although Harding Yarns was not part of the Canadian yarn scene for long, some knitters never forgot them.

Canadian knitters enjoyed testing their knitting skills at the CNE and other exhibitions. They entered their work year after year and record numbers of prizes were awarded. A letter of appreciation from one winner told everything about the proper attitude of the sporting knitter:

Once again I am very happy indeed to be a prize winner; being awarded second prize for a man's grey sleeveless sweater makes me very happy. I like to knit and am very encouraged by the number of prizes I have been awarded from time to time.

Thanking you very much for my award, and the safe return of my entries, and the receipt of a cheque for three dollars; I am looking forward to entering again next year.[69]

Design Contests

In the past, excellence of workmanship was emphasized, and knitters were often rewarded for perfect execution of someone else's design. Today, a higher premium is placed on originality and uniqueness of design while still insisting on sound knitting technique. Some enterprising organizations have provided Canadian knitters with excellent opportunities to demonstrate their splendid talent for design.

In 1984, White Buffalo Mills challenged knitters from across Canada to create unique garments from its spun and unspun pure wool yarns, and it offered the winners unprecedented prize money. The contest entry form provided a fully-sized graph style pattern for a foundation but also gave many opportunities for innovation.

"Good luck and happy knitting!" was wished to each contest entrant. The first-prize winner created a unique jacket and overvest ensemble that set a new standard for outdoor dressing in Canada, a look which has since been often imitated.

In 1985, The Vancouver *Sun*, in cooperation with Patons & Baldwins Ltd., gave its readers an opportunity to do their very best knitting for exciting and worthwhile prizes like a trip for two to England. The *Sun* provided a basic one-size-fits-all unisex sweater pattern that knitters could recreate in any yarn, using any trimming technique they desired, while ensuring that the finished product conformed to the correct measurements.

British Columbia's knitters pulled out all the stops for this contest, producing embroidered,

First prize winner in the White Buffalo Mills design contest

appliqued, and pearl encrusted sweaters of great beauty. They proved that Canada's home knitters have talents that are unrivalled in the professional knitting design world.

Entries were judged on "originality, design, and workmanship." The first-prize winner was a pale peach extravaganza of intricate beadwork in a wisteria design.

Another winner captured the imagination of knitters and non-knitters alike for it was a representation of the Vancouver skyline with the Expo centre embossed on the front of the sweater. A finer example of commemorative knitting has seldom been seen. The "Expo sweater," as it came to be known, featured more than ten different yarns and was worked in astonishing textures, colours, and shapes. It became a symbol of civic pride and of the general happiness of that glorious summer of Expo '86 in Vancouver.

Until recent years, knitting played but little part in juried craft exhibitions. Quilting, weaving, and embroidery were all recognized as textile art forms, but knitting, an equally demanding and challenging craft medium, was ignored in professional circles. The tide has turned and more knitted masterpieces find their way into galleries and museum collections every year. Anne MacLeod

Prado's intricate sweater named "A Nova Scotian Yarn" is a fine example of knitted art that has received recognition in the wider artistic world. It was designated Curator's Choice in the recent Nova Scotia Designer Crafts Council exhibition titled *PatterNS: Applied & Implied* and became the promotional symbol of this unique show. The designer spent several months working out graphed images, colour combinations, and stitch calculations on paper before she cast on a single stitch.

Canadian knitters are very skillful and nothing stimulates our creative juices like a design competition that promises praises or prizes. It brings out the best in us as a knitting nation, challenging our artistic abilities and confirming our world-class talent as knitters. It moves knitting out of the precinct of the living room and puts it into the pages of national magazines, into galleries, and into private collections where it gets the recognition it deserves.

Knitting Canada Together

Yarn companies, the media, and arts and crafts organizations have been instrumental in bringing

"A Nova Scotian Yarn" by Anne MacLeod Prado. This handsome sweater was designated "Curators Choice" in the 1988 PatterNS juried exhibition, sponsored by the Nova Scotia Designer Crafts Council.

knitting to the attention of the wider world, but individual knitters who love their art have also made some astonishing personal contributions.

Christine Harrison of Oakville, Ontario, is a knitter who loves Canada as much as her art and who accordingly named her business the Great Canadian Believer company. A former professional figure skater, Christine had toured the world and realized that abroad Canada is known for the beauty of our country — and for the beauty of our knitting. She decided to personally organize a gala fashion show that would showcase Canada's hand-knitting talent as never before. She called her show Knitting Canada Together and it did just that.

Christine had a prophet's sense of mission toward knitting in Canada and knew how to do things right. The show was held on October 18, 1986, and featured professional choreography and expert commentary. She organized contributions of original hand-knit sweaters from each of Canada's provinces and territories. Some of these beauties were themselves the winners of contests in their own home districts. Creations like the Indian Ceremonial Button Robe from British Columbia and the Riding into the Sunset sweater from Saskatchewan were unique pieces that celebrated the diversity of Canadian life through the medium of knitting. More than one hundred original hand knits were modelled and later bought by enthusiastic patrons. Newspapers lauded Christine's efforts and politicians endorsed them. She knit Canada together.

Christine is just one of many private individuals who have given their time and money in great abundance for no other reason than their love of knitting and their desire to see it recognized.

Competition, civic pride, the joy of creation, and the desire to excel are human qualities that Canadian knitters seem to possess in extra measure.

Knitting for Peace

Canadians have knit for glory, for pleasure, and for profit. They have also knit for peace. During the Vietnam War, more than 30,000 items were knit for the children of Vietnamese civilians left homeless by the conflict. Knitters with a social conscience were challenged to make their work count in a way that it never had before.

This unparalleled knitting effort was organized by the Voice of Women for Peace. The Voice of Women, a voluntary non-partisan organization with members in every province of Canada, was founded in 1960 to oppose violence and to promote disarmament and peace. VOW's efforts to end the war in Vietnam and to provide humanitarian aid to its victims led to exchanges of visits with Vietnamese women and to the Ontario Voice of Women Knitting Project, an unusual knitting effort that lasted ten years.

The request for knitted children's clothing originally came from the Children's Committee of the Canadian Aid for Vietnamese Civilians, a movement headquartered in Vancouver. This group was the first to make known the need for warm clothing for the victims of war who were sometimes forced to live in caves after their villages were destroyed.

The first clothing shipment contained a mere thirty-four garments, knit by a handful of concerned women; however, the VOW did a tremendous job of publicizing its cause, and commitment accelerated rapidly. Later shipments contained as many as two thousand items made by fifteen hundred different knitters. The work was done by members of the Y.W.C.A., trade union auxiliaries, the Brownies and Girl Guides, high school groups, senior citizens, the Elizabeth Fry Sisterhood, and volunteers from many church groups.

Garments were collected at the Toronto home of Lil Greene, convenor of the Ontario Voice of Women Knitting Project for Vietnamese Children and a concerned and experienced peace worker. Parcels were sent from Toronto to Vancouver where they were transported on Soviet ships to Haiphong. Once in Vietnam, they were distributed by the Red Cross.

The knitting project turned a number of committed middle-class women into masters of the art of public relations. They became very good at getting publicity for their work. The knitting project was written about in dozens of major newspapers, in publications like the *United Church Observer*, and in trade union communications and was even filmed for television. The Voice of Women had a booth at the Canadian National Exhibition for many years. Coverage of the knitting project in a U.S. newspaper brought in thousands of knitted garments from Americans who put the cause of suffering children above the requirements of their government.

The Voice of Women marched in demonstrations and protested in shopping malls. Members held teas and public meetings. They also made a memorable train trip to Ottawa on April 18, 1970, to protest Canada's complicity in the war in Vietnam. A knitted blanket was begun as the train

Volunteers for the Ontario Voice of Women Knitting Project
pack garments to be sent to civilians in Vietnam in 1970.
Garments were knit in dark colours for camouflage.

pulled out of Toronto and throughout the trip fellow passengers were invited to knit a few rows and sign a petition for peace.

VOW communications bore two symbols — the dove of peace and the drawing of a clothesline full of tiny babies' clothes. When the group marched together, they carried a real clothesline with baby clothes and they became instantly identifiable among protest groups.

A sign reading "Dark Colours for Camouflage" hung from the clothesline too. "Dark Colours for Camouflage" became the sobering watchword of the knitting project, evoking all the horror of helpless civilians faced with a powerful enemy. One article made the reason for dark colours explicit. "A baby wrapped in a bright shawl or garment is a deadly attraction for napalm or high explosive bombs," it cautioned.[70]

Patterns, yarn, and support were supplied by the Voice of Women. The most needed garments were bootees, vests, shawls, balaclavas, and cot blankets made up of knitted squares. Less accomplished knitters were invited to make simple garter stitch squares, which were later joined together to make blankets. Regular newsletters provided encouragement and kept knitters on track. One of these read:

NOW THE SQUARES — Please remember that Asians always hang out their bedding each day; also sometimes the babies do not have adequate cover from flares dropped for bombings. These flares pick up white and light colours very quickly. It is so hard for us to realize just how dangerously these people are living and how, from day to day, millions of them must be alert for air raids.

Every knitter for the Ontario Voice of Women Knitting Project received a personal letter of thanks. By 1973, the international situation had changed and knitters could once again use bright colours in their children's clothing, but they did not stop knitting until 1975/76 when the war ended. The war may have come to an end, but the Voice of Women has never stopped working for peace.

The Ontario Voice of Women booth at the Canadian National Exhibition.

Knitting and Good Works

Some knitters work to raise monuments to their faith and their beliefs, lasting legacies for future generations. Others simply want to help the needy along the difficult path of life. Throughout Canadian history, the humble knitting needle has often been an instrument of good works.

Turkey Teas and Sales of Work

When our foremothers wanted to raise money for some worthy cause, they did not prepare a brochure, a telephone tree, or a mailing list. As often as not, they took up their needles and began to knit. Canadians would be truly astonished if they could tally up the number of churches built, the number of missionaries supported, and the number of homeless clothed with money made from knitting.

From the community gatherings known as "turkey teas" in Newfoundland to the church bazaars and suppers of the prairies, the custom of holding sales of work to raise money is Canada-wide. Two stories from Nova Scotia are illustrations of the role that knitting has played in fundraising and in building programmes in past centuries. In some cases, the knitters who sought to raise money would have seemed to our latter-day eyes to be rather in need of it themselves.

Seal Island is a small island off the southwestern tip of Nova Scotia. Its location, tides, fogs, and currents make it a particularly treacherous place. Champlain was the first to pronounce it dangerous when he passed by on his early voyages. Hundreds of lives had been lost off its inhospitable shores until a life-saving station was established there in the middle of the nineteenth century.

Unpredictable and often hazardous weather conditions made it very difficult for any minister to reach the island, but its inhabitants yearned for their own church. Mrs. Winifred Crowell Hamilton, who lived on the island all her life, remembered her mother's longing for a place of worship and the steps she and her neighbours took to satisfy it.

Sitting down in one of the rounded back chairs her thoughts took her back to the living room of the old house, [herself] a child playing with her toys in the corner while her mother and neighbouring women pieced quilts together,

knit mittens, caps and socks and did fancy work around the Ottawa heater, to sell at the annual lawn party and supper each spring to raise money to build a church. For years her mother had dreamed of having their own church on the hill overlooking the East shore, a place of worship where the Islanders could gather together in a building set aside for worship...[71]

After thousands of stitches had been knit and seven hundred dollars painstakingly collected, the church was built. Knitting was the means by which one woman achieved the selfless desire of her devout heart.

The thought of knitting does not often cross the minds of politicians. In the early decades of the nineteenth century in Nova Scotia, Joseph Howe, one of the greatest statesmen and populist leaders in that province's colourful history, spoke out for knitting. The occasion was a threatened withdrawal of public funds from Acadia College, now Acadia University, an institution that was then closely affiliated with the Baptist Church. Speaking about the threatened well-being of Acadia in the House of Assembly, Joseph Howe warned:

You may withdraw your public money but there will be more socks and mittens knit on the hills of Wilmot, more tubs of butter made, more fat calves killed and more missionary travellers sent through the country and Acadia College will stand on the hillside in spite of the withdrawal of the grant ...[72]

Few politicians have better appreciated the nature of the economic underpinnings of the institutions of their day and of the contribution that women made to them.

"A Little Bridge from the Island of Waste to the Island of Want": Knitting With A Mission

"If only a little bridge could be thrown from the Island of Waste to the Island of Want how both would benefit," mused Lady Wolverton of Irwene, Dorset, England; and she immediately began to build that bridge by founding the Needlework Guild in 1882. A mere ten years later, the Toronto branch of the Needlework Guild of Canada was formed to help implement Lady Wolverton's great vision. It is still in operation today.

Lady Wolverton's original concern was for the victims of a mine disaster in Wales. She was particularly devoted to providing clothing for children left orphaned and homeless by the disaster. When she explained her mission to other women it was in these terms:

"I'm asking you for two new articles of clothing. They must be new. They must be exactly alike."

"But why two garments?" she was asked.

"What does the child wear while what he has been wearing is being laundered?" replied Lady Wolverton with great practicality.

These are still the guidelines of the Needlework Guild of Canada today, although now the two articles need not be identical. Its objective is to collect and distribute new garments for adults and children.

The Guild consists of a number of working groups, each with its own convenor and associates. An individual's annual contribution of two or more new articles of clothing constitutes membership in a group. These groups meet on their own terms and are sometimes centred around a particular church or neighbourhood.

Once a year, on the officially designated Distribution Day, all of the garments are gathered up and presented to charitable organizations such as the Children's Aid Society, women's shelters, missions, and hospitals. In order to make certain that organizations get what they require and can best use, they submit an order in advance of Distribution Day.

Matching the knitting abilities of a group of volunteers to the clothing needs of a group of strangers is always a great challenge so the Guild supplies yarn, patterns, and suggestions. A recent call went out for clothes for the homeless, the disabled, and for babies. The Guild wrote:

A particular need has been mentioned for men's mitts, knitted toques and scarves. The preemie bonnets and booties have been an overwhelming success, particularly in the largest size where the need is greatest. Perhaps some of you might like to consider baby sweaters in the newborn to 3 month size as an alternative project. However, we still need all those other wonderful items you all make each year; children's mitts, hats and sweaters, socks, lap size afghans for the disabled, bed socks, bed jackets or shawls for the elderly, scarves etc. Do keep your needles busy. The need is so great.

In a nation of plenty, the magnitude of this clothing drive is prodigious. In 1988, for example, 5,795 articles were distributed to nineteen different agencies. In response to a request by Toronto's Women's College Hospital alone, 765 bonnets and 289 pairs of booties for premature babies were supplied. These statistics are a rather disturbing reminder of the continuing presence of want in our land of wealth.

Many other groups also continue the tradition of committed knitting. The I.O.D.E deserves special mention. Its sense of mission is born of its long experience that grew strong in wartime. Absence of conflict has not extinguished its work, and it provides layettes to public health nurses and hospitals across Canada. Some chapters have adopted entire schools in their own provinces or in areas where the need is greater, and they take on the obligation of providing each child with a pair of mitts or a toque. One province provides its members with a knitting pattern per month, a strategy that has proved very popular in securing the most needed garments and in providing variety for the knitters. In 1989 alone, the I.O.D.E. spent more than $400,000 on clothing and bedding, which included mitts, baby sets, lap robes, afghans, and other knitted items.

The Red Cross, the Canadian National Institute for the Blind, and the Canadian Save the Children Fund are but a few of the higher profile agencies that also knit with a mission. In a day when good money can be made by knitting and our motives often focus on knitting for profit, we salute their selfless efforts. It seems that while knitting has moved from the realm of necessity to the realm of novelty, necessity is still with us.

The Knitting Way to Enlightenment

Whether knitting for necessity or for novelty, for warmth or for creative fulfillment, Canadians in all centuries have known the joy of knitting, the pleasure of having the yarn slip smoothly through the fingers, and the satisfaction of seeing fine fabric formed by adding row upon row of magical stitching.

Not only is knitting joyous but it also has an indisputable therapeutic effect; some say because its rhythmic motions echo the beat of the human heart. In 1914, Lucy Maud Montgomery wrote in her diary:

There have been so many days lately that I could do absolutely nothing, not even read, because my nerves got in such a state. Now, knitting has always had a good effect on me when I am nervous. I was always very fond of knitting and I find that it helps me greatly these bad days.[73]

In our own times, women like Vera Turner have come to know the therapeutic benefits of yarn and needles. When her husband died a year or so ago, Vera knit fifteen or more glorious sweaters — and gave them all away to friends and relatives. Both the giving and the receiving were emotional catharses for all concerned. The sweaters meant so much more than the simple materials from which they were made.

Even discouraged knitters still acknowledge the psychological benefits of their craft. They agree with Lucy Maud Montgomery who said, "Well, after all, it gave me pleasure in the making and so what matters if the result was not worth while? I had 'the joy of the working' and that was the essence of heaven."

Knitters worldwide share these same strong feelings about their art even though they may not share a common language. In fact, far from being a passive pastime, knitting is a dynamic thread that connects us to cultures and times very distant from our own. The great master knitter Elizabeth Zimmermann explained the deeply satisfying experience of cultural immersion through knitting.

Many years ago I was provided with genuine Irish instructions, and permitted to make the first Aran sweater I had ever seen or heard of, for Vogue Pattern Book...I puzzled over the directions, which included no picture of what I was actually making, the unaccustomed terms of back twist and forward twist made themselves gradually at home in my brain, the oiled wool slipped through my fingers, "...the sun beat down upon it all, and thus my dream began". Not quite a dream, but a strong feeling that my fingers knew quite well what they were about, and welcomed the chance to be about it again after a long lapse of time. I knew then that I had been through this before, with younger fingers in a ruder boat, rocked on the salty summer waves of the Atlantic off the Irish coast." [74]

Still other knitters find the siren call of present and future knitting more seductive than the call of the past. They want to forge ahead with civilization and to break new aesthetic ground. They want their exuberant creations to communicate the vitality of today's rich world.

Hand knitting is a part of the Canadian consciousness, in happiness and in hardship, in family memories and civic celebrations. With skill and vision, today's knitters can explore our new cultural horizons or deepen our contact with our own Canadian roots. The choice is ours and the times and materials have never been more inviting.

Notes

1. Some examples of French painting showing women working with wool are "Figures in a Landscape" by Michael Ancher, 1880, "The Netmender" by Christian Krohg, 1879, and "Breton Peasant Knitting" by Roderick O'Connor, 1893. Reproductions are published in the book *The Good and Simple Life: Artists Colonies in Europe and America* by Michael Jacobs, Oxford: Phaidon Press, 1985.

2. Rutt, *A History of Hand Knitting*, 67.

3. Moodie, *Roughing it in the Bush, or, Life in Canada*, 92.

4. Ibid., 157.

5. Ibid., 502.

6. Ibid., 501.

7. Johnston, *Westworld*, 53.

8. Harrington, *Canadian Geographical Journal*, 95.

9. Barrett, *Them Days*, 41–42.

10. Johnston, *Grenfell of Labrador*, 142.

11. Thoms, *Born to Serve*, 3.

12. Ibid., 3.

13. Ibid., 5.

14. Ibid., 6.

15. Green, *Don't Have Your Baby in the Dory!*, 76.

16. Ibid., 113.

17. Ibid., 109.

18. Ibid., 64.

19. "The NONIA Way." *Decks Awash Magazine*, 56–57.

20. Gough, *The Art of David Blackwood*, n.p.

21. Story, *Dictionary of Newfoundland English*, 128.

22. Dexter, *Traditional Nova Scotian Double-Knitting Patterns*, 2.

23. Hansen, *Flying Geese & Partridge Feet*, 20.

24. Pocius, *Textile Traditions of Eastern Newfoundland*, 23.

25. Payne, Mrs. Edgar, Letter to the author dated January 11, 1990.

26. Hansen, *Fox & Geese & Fences*, 20.

27. Courtesy of Winterhouses.

28. Montgomery, *Selected Journals*, 1:75.

29. Foster, *Annapolis Valley Saga*, 86.

30. Richardson, *We Keep A Light*, 92.

31. Ibid., 92.

32. Ibid., 92.

33. Ibid., 92.

34. Story, 593.

35. Newman, *Empire of the Bay*, 182.

36. Richardson, 90.

37. Payne, Letter to the author.

38. Richardson, 91.

39. Story, 211.

40. Ibid., 211.

41. Gough, n.p.

42. Ibid., n.p.

43. Minutes of the National Council meeting, Navy League of Canada, 1943.

44. *Knit! Knit! Knit! For the Navy and Merchant Navy*, n.d., 11.

45. Moodie, 116.

46. *The Canadian Mother and Child*, 95.

47. Zimmermann, *Knitter's Almanac*, 17.

48. Adams, *Macleans Magazine*, 22.

49. Guy, *Atlantic Insight*, June 1989, 42.

50. Georgia, *An Arctic Diary*, 46.

51. Moodie, 221.

52. Montgomery, 2:143.

53. Carrier, *The Hockey Sweater*, 77.

54. Hyde, *National Geographic*, 554.

55. Guy, *Atlantic Insight*, December 1988, 50.

56. Conrad, *No Place Like Home*, 72.

57. Foster, *Annapolis Valley Saga*, 111.

58. Schell, *The Musk-Ox Underwool, Qiviut*, 13.

59. *Chatelaine*, February 1934.

60. Robb, *Chatelaine*, September 1937, 22.

61. *Canadian Living*, April 16, 1988, 124.

62. Rutt, 62.

63. Smith, *The Wealth of Nations*, 110.

64. *The Workwoman's Guide*, 237.

65. Barrett, 41.

66. Rutt, 17.

67. Gough, n.p.

68. Murray, *More Than 50%*, 27.

69. Correspondence of Elsa Jenkins, courtesy CNE Archives.

70. Ontario Voice of Women communiqué, n.d.

71. Hichens, *Island Trek*, 20.

72. Dennis, *Down in Nova Scotia*, 81.

73. Montgomery, 2:143.

74. Zimmermann, 76.

Bibliography

Adams, Eric R. "Born to Mr. & Mrs. Canada 300,000 Babies." *Macleans Magazine*, May 15, 1947, 22.

Agriculture Canada. *Wool Production in Canada.* Publication 1763/E. Ottawa: Ministry of Supply and Services, 1984.

Barrett, Harriet. "Things We Had, We Made." *Them Days*, March 1985, 41– 43.

Bennett, Helen. *Scottish Knitting.* Aylesbury, Bucks, UK: Shire Publications Ltd., 1986.

Braden, Bill. "Weaving a Northern Legend." *Up Here: Life in Canada's North*, October/November 1985, 28–29.

Branch, Stephen N. "Briggs & Little: The Yarn Makers." *Canadian Textile Journal*, January 1982, 33–35.

Brothers, Ryan. "Cowichan Knitters." *The Beaver: Magazine of the North*, Summer 1965, 42–46.

"Canada's swetter boy gits hisself a noo nit: Charlie Farquharson's favrit cardygun is so aynchunt it's in vague again." *Canadian Living*, April 16, 1988, 124–133.

The Canadian Mother and Child. Ottawa: Department of National Health and Welfare, 1961.

Carrier, Roch. *The Hockey Sweater and Other Stories.* Translated by Sheila Fischman. Toronto: House of Anansi Press, 1979.

Chambers, Wendy. "Cowichan Knitting Industry." *Heddle: A Canadian Publication for Spinners and Weavers*, 2, no.4 (November/December 1985, January 1986): 32– 33.

Conrad, Margaret, Toni Laidlaw, and Donna Smyth, comps. *No Place Like Home: Diaries and Letters of Nova Scotia Women 1771– 1938.* Halifax: Formac, 1988.

Dennis, Clara. *Down in Nova Scotia.* Toronto: Ryerson Press, 1934.

Dexter, Janetta. *Traditional Nova Scotian Double-Knitting Patterns.* Halifax: Nova Scotia Museum, 1985.

"English Accents." *Vogue Knitting International.* Holiday, 1988, 40– 44.

Fallis, Donna. "World War I Knitting." *Alberta Museums Review*, Fall, 1984.

Foster, Malcolm Cecil. *Annapolis Valley Saga.* Windsor, Nova Scotia: Lancelot Press, 1976.

Gainford, Veronica. *Designs for Knitting Kilt Hose and Knickerbocker Stockings.* Published by the author. Argyll, Scotland, 1978.

Georgia. *An Arctic Diary.* Edmonton: Hurtig, 1982.

Gibson-Roberts, Priscilla. "Qiviut — the ultimate luxury fibre." *Knitter's Magazine*, Fall 1987, 58– 59.

Gibson-Roberts, Priscilla and Margaret Meikle. "Big and Bold — the Cowichan Style." *Knitter's Magazine*, Fall/Winter 1986, 60– 65.

Gordon, Joleen. "Knitting." In *A Nova Scotia Work Basket: Some Needlework Patterns Traditionally Used in the Province.* Halifax: Nova Scotia Museum, 1976.

Gough, William. *The Art of David Blackwood.* Toronto: McGraw-Hill Ryerson Limited, 1988.

Green, H. Gordon. *Don't Have Your Baby in the Dory! A Biography of Myra Bennett.* Montreal: Harvest House, 1973.

Gushue, John. "Clouds Over Fishery Have Silver Lining for Rural Crafts Industry." *The Sunday Express*, St. John's Newfoundland, July 9, 1989.

Guy, Ray. "Ba-DAY-das of a Day Gone By." *Atlantic Insight*, June 1989, 42.

———."Mysteries of the Wider World." *Atlantic Insight*, December 1988, 50.

Hansen, Robin. *Fox & Geese & Fences: Traditional Maritime & Maine Mittens.* Halifax: Formac, 1983.

Hansen, Robin, with Janetta Dexter. *Flying Geese & Partridge Feet: More Mittens From Up North and Down East.* Camden, Maine: Down East Books, 1986.

Harrington, Lyn. "The Cowichan Sweater." *Canadian Geographical Journal* XL (1950): 94– 95.

Harvey, Michael. *Patons: A Story of Handknitting.* Ascot, England: Springwood Books Ltd., 1985.

Hichens, Walter W. *Island Trek.* Hantsport, Nova Scotia: Lancelot Press, 1982.

Hobbs, Anna. "Cowichan Indian Sweaters: The Warm, Wonderful Status Symbol." *Canadian Living,* September 1982, 41– 46.

———."A Royal Pair: Knit the Cowichans Charles & Di Wear." *Canadian Living,* September 1982, 95–104.

———."From Ewe to You." *Canadian Living,* September 1988, 108 –112.

Hollingworth, Shelagh. *Knitting and Crochet for the Physically Handicapped and Elderly.* London: Batsford, 1981.

Hooray for Canada. Toronto: Telemedia Publishing, 1989.

Hyde, Nina. "Wool: Fabric of History." *National Geographic Magazine* 173, no. 5 (1988): 552 –591.

Johnston, James. *Grenfell of Labrador.* London: S.W. Partridge, n.d.

Johnston, O. L. "Jeremina Colvin's Gift to the Cowichans." *Westworld,* March/April 1976, 53–54.

Kee, Nancy Erb. "The Incredible Mrs. A," in *Once Upon a Century: 100 Year History of the "Ex."* Toronto: J. H. Robinson Publishing Ltd., 1978.

Kerkhoven, Marijke. *Analysis of Textile Crafts at Selected Agricultural Fairs in Alberta and Saskatchewan, 1879 –1915.* M.Sc. thesis, University of Alberta, 1986.

Knit! Knit! Knit! For the Navy and Merchant Navy. Toronto: Navy League of Canada, 1940.

"Knitwear Architects." *Knitter's Magazine* 15 (Summer 1989): 13 –16.

Lane, Barbara. "The Cowichan Knitting Industry." *Anthropology in B.C.* Victoria: Provincial Museum, 1951, 14– 27.

Lees, Judi and Chris Potter. "The Inside Story." *Your Money,* July/August 1987.

Ligon, Linda, ed. *Homespun, Handknit: Caps, Socks, Mittens and Gloves.* Loveland, Colorado: Interweave Press, 1987.

Martin, Harriet Pardy. "Labrador Crafts: Finger Mitts." *Them Days,* 6, no. 3 (1981): 50– 51.

MacHenry, Rachel. "Converting Images into Sweaters." *Threads,* 10 (April/May 1987): 72–73.

McCoag, Tom. "Huge Demand for Dog Sweaters, Cardigans." *Chronicle-Herald/Mail Star,* Halifax, Nova Scotia, November 17, 1988.

McGrath, Judy. "Labrador Crafts." *Them Days,* June 1982, 34 – 37.

Meikle, Margaret. *Cowichan Indian Knitting.* Vancouver: UBC Museum of Anthropology, Museum Note No. 21, 1987.

Montgomery, L. M. *The Selected Journals of L. M. Montgomery.* Edited by Mary Rubio and Elizabeth Waterston. 2 vols. Toronto: University of Toronto Press, 1987.

Moodie, Susanna. *Roughing it in the Bush, or, Life in Canada.* Boston: Beacon Press, 1986. First published by Richard Bentley in 1852.

Moore, Marie. "Maritime Knitting Firm Noted for Quality Product." *The Canadian Jewish News,* January 5, 1989.

Murray, Hilda Chaulk. *More Than 50%: Woman's Life in a Newfoundland Outport 1900–1950.* St. John's, Newfoundland: Breakwater Books, 1979. (Memorial University of Newfoundland Folklore and Language Publications Monograph Series, No. 2, 1978; Canada's Atlantic Folklore and Folklife Series No. 3, 1979.)

Needlework Guild of Canada, Toronto Branch. *Annual Report for the Year Ending December 31, 1988.*

Newman, Peter C. *Empire of the Bay: An Illustrated History of the Hudson's Bay Company.* Toronto: Madison Press Books, 1989.

Nickerson, Signe. "Knitting With Handspun Canadian Wool." *Heddle: A Canadian Publication for Spinners and Weavers,* 2, no.4 (November/ December 1985, January 1986): 24.

Norcross, E. Blanche. "The Cowichan Sweater." *The Beaver,* December 1945, 18 –19.

Once Upon a Century: 100 Year History of the "Ex." Toronto: J. H. Robinson Ltd.

PatterNS: Applied & Implied. Halifax: Nova Scotia Designer Crafts Council, n.d.

Pelham, Amanda. "Cumberland County Knitters: A Nova Scotia Yarn." *Discovery,* June 1987.

Peterson, Annie S., Sarah G. Service and Helen M. Paton. *The Big Book of Needlecraft.* London: Oldhams Press, n.d., 383– 414.

Redshaw, Dorene. "Northern Fibre Artists Hook Market." *Up Here: Life in Canada's North*, April/May 1987, 15.

Richardson, Evelyn M. *The Story of the Barrington Woolen Mill*. Barrington, Nova Scotia: Cape Sable Historical Society. Reprinted from *The Journal of Education*, May/June, 1968.

———. *We Keep A Light*. Toronto: McGraw-Hill Ryerson, 1945.

Robb, Dorothy. "Your Knitting Success." *Chatelaine*, September 1937, 22–24.

Roessingh, Fen. "Custom Woolen Mills." *Heddle: A Canadian Publication for Spinners and Weavers*, 2, no.4 (November/December 1985, January 1986): 8.

Rutt, Richard. *A History of Hand Knitting*. Loveland, Colorado: Interweave Press, 1987.

Schell, Lillian Crowell. *The Musk-Ox Underwool, Qiviut: Historical Uses and Present Utilization in an Eskimo Knitting Industry*. Masters Thesis, University of Alaska, 1972.

"She Nose Style." *Up Here: Life in Canada's North*, December/January 1985, 9.

Smith, Adam. *The Wealth of Nations*. London: Penguin, 1970. Pelican Classics Edition. First published in 1776.

Story, G. M., W. J. Kirwin, and J. D. A. Widdowson, eds. *Dictionary of Newfoundland English*. Toronto: University of Toronto Press, 1982.

Templeton, Anna. *Operation Homespun*. St. John's, Newfoundland: Career Development and Advanced Studies, 1980.

"The NONIA Way." *Decks Awash Magazine* 10, no.2 (April 1981): 56–57.

The Story of Wool. The Wool Bureau of Canada, n.d.

The Workwoman's Guide. London: Simpkin, Marshall, and Co., 1840.

Thomas, Mary. *Mary Thomas's Knitting Book*. New York: Dover Publications, 1972. Originally published in 1938 by Hodder and Stoughten, Ltd.

Thoms, James R. *Born to Serve: The Story of NONIA*.

Van Tuyl, Laura. "Mittens With a Past: Folklore in the Palm of Your Hand." *Christian Science Monitor*, World Edition, January 26–February 1/89, 14.

Wallace, Birgitta Linderoth. "The L'Anse aux Meadows Site." *The Norse Atlantic Saga*. Edited by Givyn Jones. Toronto: Oxford University Press, 1986.

"Warm and Practical Classic Clothing." *Up Here: Life in Canada's North*, October/November 1987, 23.

"You Asked Us." *Vancouver Sun*, Jan 28, 1989.

Zimmermann, Elizabeth. *Elizabeth Zimmermann's Knitter's Almanac: Projects for Each Month of the Year*. New York: Dover Publications, 1974.

Photo Credits

3: Photo by W. Sturge, courtesy of the Department of Development, Promotion Services, Government of Newfoundland and Labrador. 8: Photo by Richard Harrington, National Archives of Canada/PA 139226. 10: Courtesy of Sasquatch Trading Ltd. 11: Ryan Collection, Provincial Archives of B.C./HP96363. 12: Photo by Malak, National Archives of Canada/PA 150163. 13: Photo by Bill Dennett/Vancouver *Sun*, National Archives of Canada/PA 139227. 14: Courtesy of Sasquatch Trading Ltd. 15: Photo by Kate Hettasch, courtesy of *Them Days* Magazine. 21: Courtesy of David Blackwood. 22: Photo by A. Turkington. 24: Courtesy of the Royal Ontario Museum. 25: Photo by A. Turkington. 27: upper, PANS N-5408 Dennis Collection; left, PANS N-5403 Dennis Collection; right, PANS N-5412 Dennis Collection; courtesy of the Public Archives of Nova Scotia. 29: National Archives of Canada/C22217. 30: left, National Archives of Canada/C53064; right, Courtesy of the Hockey Hall of Fame. 31: left, National Archives of Canada/PA 138589; right, National Archives of Canada/C-4666. 33: Courtesy of the Canadian War Museum/Musée canadienne de la guerre. 36: National Archives of Canada/PA 105612. 38: Courtesy of Patons & Baldwins. 39: Photo by Bollinger, Public Archives of Nova Scotia/655 C. 41: Lady Fair Book of Children's Wear, 1927. 43: Courtesy of Patons & Baldwins Canada. 44: Courtesy of A. Turkington. 45: Courtesy of the CNE Archives. 47: Photo by Patons Design Studio, Book 526, "O Canada," courtesy of Patons & Baldwins Canada. 49: Courtesy of Patons & Baldwins Canada. 52: Notman Photographic Archives, McCord Museum of Canadian History/177,709-II. 54: Patons & Baldwins Canada. 56: Courtesy of Canadian Parks Service. 58: Courtesy of Patons & Baldwins Canada. 62: National Archives of Canada/PA 98827. 63: Courtesy of the Sports Hall of Fame. 64: Courtesy of the Whyte Museum of the Canadian Rockies/NA 66-1382. 65: Courtesy of Mary Maxim Ltd. 74: Courtesy of Spinrite Yarns. 76: National Archives of Canada/PA 44848. 77: Photo by B. Timney, courtesy of Brian Timney. 79: Courtesy of R. Stone. 80: Courtesy of C. MacPhee. 82: Courtesy of Wendy Chambers. 83: Photo by Richard Harrington, courtesy of Richard Harrington and Wendy Chambers. 87: Courtesy of Wool City International. 89: Courtesy of Craft Cottage. 90: bottom, Courtesy of Village Yarns. 94: Courtesy of Mrs. Edgar Payne. 95: left and right, Courtesy of the New Brunswick Museum. 97: Courtesy of Russell O'Brien. 98: Courtesy of Don Colvin. 99: Courtesy of Mark Radigan. 100: Notman Photographic Archives, McCord Museum of Canadian History. 102: Courtesy of the 4-H project "Working With Wool," Ontario Ministry of Agriculture and Food. 103: Courtesy of Montgomery's Inn. 104: Courtesy of Harmony Classics. 105: Photo by Studio Focus 21, courtesy of Linda Laing. 106: Courtesy of Knitwear Architects. 107: lower left, Photo by John Panagiotopolous, courtesy of Rachel MacHenry. 108: lower left, courtesy of Lynn Maclachlan. 109: Courtesy of Whale Cove Knitters. 110: Photo by Wayne MacDonald, courtesy of Cumberland County Knitters. 112: Courtesy of Mary Maxim Ltd. 113: Courtesy of the CNE Archives. 115: Courtesy of White Buffalo Mills. 116: Photo by George Georgakakos, courtesy of the Nova Scotia Designer Crafts Council and Anne MacLeod Prado. 118: Photo by McLorinan, courtesy of the *Globe and Mail.* 119: Courtesy of Lil Greene.

Photo Section I

2: top, Photo by N. Rodrigues, courtesy of the Arctic Coast Tourist Association; bottom, Courtesy of the New Brunswick Department of Tourism. 3: Photo by Lyn Hancock, courtesy of Lyn Hancock. 4: top, Courtesy of Mary Maxim Ltd.; bottom, Photo by Jim Stephens, reprinted, by permission, *Canadian Living* Magazine. 5: Photo by Jim Allen, reprinted, by permission, *Canadian Living* Magazine. 6: top, Courtesy of Patons & Baldwins; bottom, Courtesy of Wool City International. 7: top, Courtesy of C. Harrison; bottom, Photo by Wayne MacDonald, courtesy of Cumberland County Knitters. 8: Photo by D. Florkow.

Photo Section II

1: Courtesy of L. Maclachlan. 2: top, Photo by A. Turkington, courtesy of Patons & Baldwins; bottom, Courtesy of M. Mulroney. 4: top, Photo by John Panagiotopolous, courtesy of R. MacHenry; bottom, Courtesy of Candace Carter. 5: top, Photo by Wolfgang Weber, courtesy of Travel Arctic, Government of the N.W.T.; bottom, Courtesy of Campbell Soup Co. 6: top, Courtesy of Patons & Baldwins; bottom, Photo by John Stephens, reprinted, by permission, *Canadian Living* Magazine. 7: bottom, Courtesy of Harmony Classics. 8: Courtesy of the Wool Bureau of Canada.